CONTENTS

Section 1
Exercises

Section 2
Exercises

Section 3
Exercises

Section 4
Exercises

Section 1

CSPE

Exercise 1: Survival Island

We must have certain needs met in order to survive. What would you bring to this desert island to help you survive?

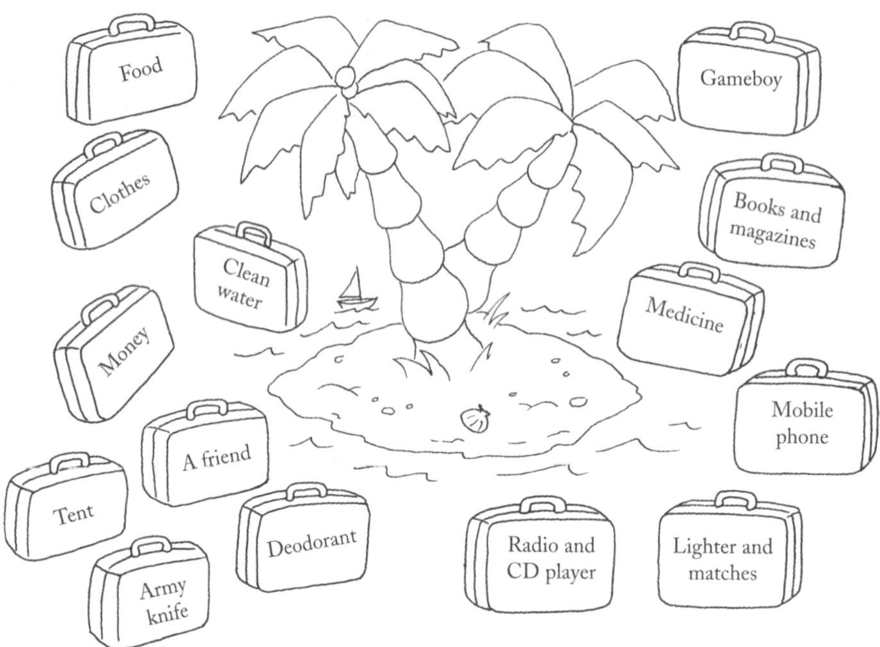

1. Choose four items written on the suitcases and write your choices in the blank suitcases.

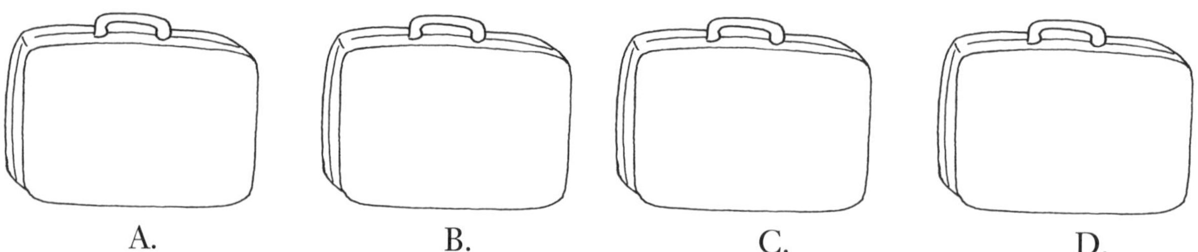

2. Explain the reasons for your choices.

   Reason A: ________________________________

   Reason B: ________________________________

   Reason C: ________________________________

   Reason D: ________________________________

3. What is the difference between a want and a need? Explain your answer.

   ____

   ____

Exercise 2: The Rights Picture

The United Nations Declaration of Human Rights names rights that every person should have. Below is a list of some of those rights.

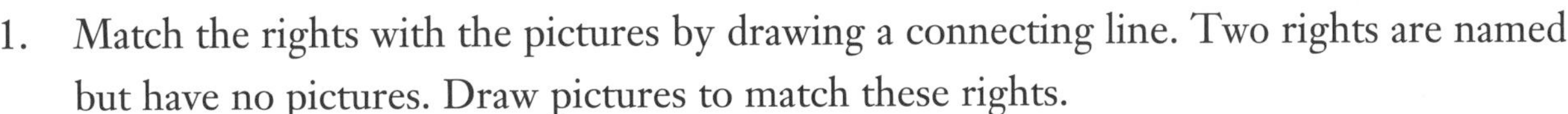

1. Match the rights with the pictures by drawing a connecting line. Two rights are named but have no pictures. Draw pictures to match these rights.

a) 

b)  

c)

d)

e) 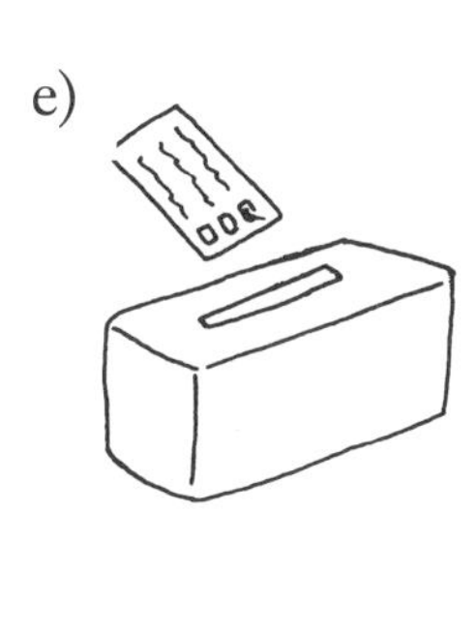

f)  

g)

h) 

i) *The right to leisure and rest*

ii) *The right to marry*

iii) *The right to have food*

iv) *The right to health care*

v) *The right to an education*

vi) *The right to equal treatment before the courts*

vii) *The right to vote*

viii) *The right to shelter*

2. Name another set of rights drawn up by the United Nations.

____

Exercise 3: Children's Rights

Look at the United Nations Convention on the Rights of the Child. These rights are separated into four main areas.

Development Rights
Play
Education
Cultural activities
To speak your own language

Survival Rights
Food
Clean water
Shelter
Medicine/health care

UN CONVENTION ON THE RIGHTS OF THE CHILD

Participation Rights
To take an active part in society
To express your opinion
To meet together and express your views

Protection Rights
To be kept safe and not be hurt
Not to be used as cheap labour
Not to be used as a child soldier

1. From each of the four areas named above circle the right you think is most important.

2. Draw a picture of each right you have chosen and explain why it is important.

a) *Development Right*

This right is important because ____________

____

____

____

____

____

____

____

____

b) *Survival Right*

This right is important because ____________

____

____

____

____

____

____

____

____

c) *Participation Right*

This right is important because ____________

____

____

____

____

____

____

____

____

d) *Protection Right*

This right is important because ____________

____

____

____

____

____

____

____

____

Exercise 4: Hand in Hand

Having rights also means having responsibilities.

Example: Everyone has the right to a clean environment and each of us is responsible for not littering or damaging our world.

1. In the arms below fill in the missing **right** or the missing **responsibility**.

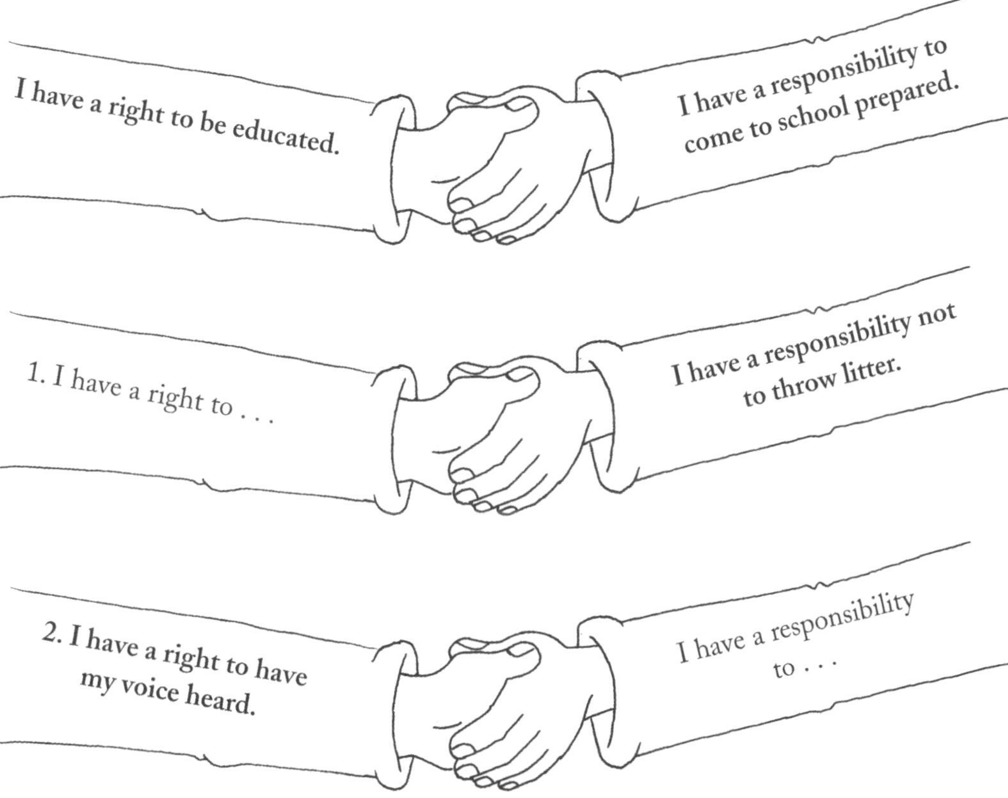

2. Name **two** rights you think are important and the responsibility that goes with each right.

Exercise 5: Is it Positive? Or is it not?

Being a member of a school community means that you have responsibilities as well as rights.

1. On the signs below, circle the actions you think are positive in **green** and the actions you think would not be OK in **red**.

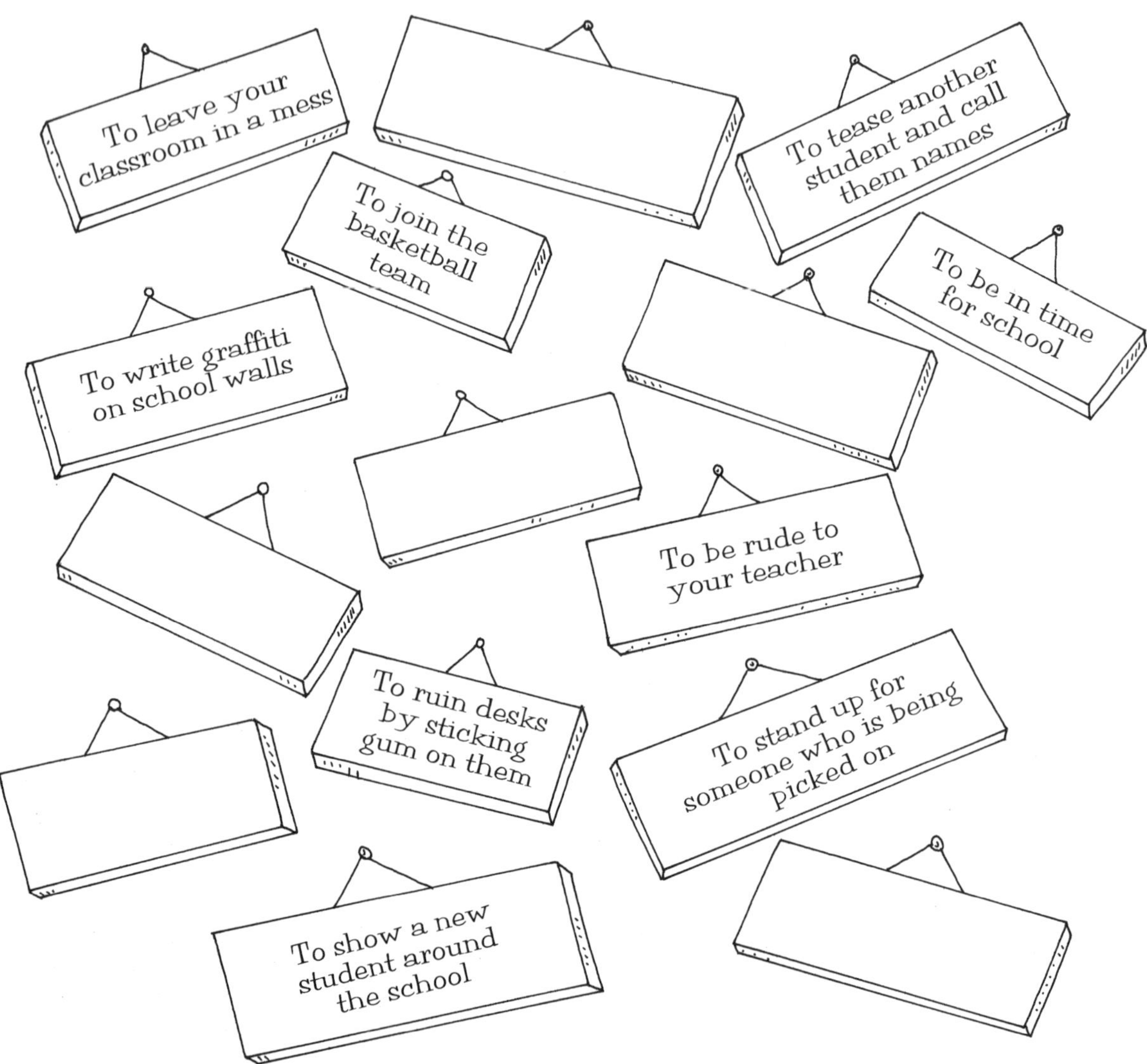

2. In the blank signs write in actions that would show you are a responsible student.

3. Explain why you think schools have rules about some of the actions you have circled in red.

____

____

Exercise 6: Bullying – No Way!

There are different kinds of bullying. Read the story below to see why going to school became difficult for this student.

> 'I hate school. I hate all the teachers. I hate all the girls. I particularly hate Maria and Alice. They raise their eyebrows and then splutter with laughter whenever I go near them. The other girls have started doing it too. And everyone groans whenever I answer in class. I can't help knowing lots. What's so bad about being clever? I wish I didn't have to go to school. Maybe I'll bunk off and creep back home and hide in the attic all day like a real Anne Frank.'
>
> Extract from Jacqueline Wilson's novel *Secrets*

1. Why do you think this girl hates school and everyone in it?

____

____

2. In this story, what kind of bullying is being carried out?

____

____

3. Why does this student feel that she is being picked on?

____

____

4. How does the girl in the story deal with the bullying?

____

____

5. Suggest another way of dealing with this problem.

____

____

6. Do you think this girl is being denied any of her rights?

____

____

Exercise 7: Your Advice

Imagine you have been asked to design an anti-bullying booklet for your school.

1. Design a front cover and slogan for your anti-bullying booklet. You could include your school name and crest on the cover.

2. Your booklet should contain information on the kinds of bullying behaviour that is **not** acceptable in your school. Outline what could be seen as bullying behaviour. Use the words in the box below to help you with your answer.

name-calling	*on-going*	*hitting and pushing*
teasing	*taking books etc.*	
spreading rumours	*repeatedly*	

3. Bullying behaviour can be:

- ______________________________
- ______________________________
- ______________________________
- ______________________________

4. Give advice on what to do if you see bullying going on.

If you see bullying going on ...

- *Refuse to join in.*
- ______________________________
- ______________________________
- ______________________________
- ______________________________
- ______________________________

5. Give advice on what to do if you are being bullied.

If you are being bullied ...

- *Tell a teacher.*
- ______________________________
- ______________________________
- ______________________________
- ______________________________
- ______________________________

Exercise 8: Who does What?

There are many organisations that support and raise awareness of the rights of others in society.

1. Match the organisations listed below with the issue that concerns them. There may be more than one organisation that is concerned with the same issue.

Concern/Issue	Organisation
1. Homelessness	A, J
2. Refugees	
3. The Developing World	
4. Poverty in Irish Society	
5. The Needs of the Elderly	
6. Care of the Environment	
7. Child Welfare	
8. Animal Welfare	

Organisations

A. Focus Ireland
B. ACTIONAID Ireland
C. Age Action Ireland
D. Alone
E. Barnardos
F. Concern Worldwide
G. Goal
H. Irish Red Cross Society
I. Irish Refugee Council
J. Simon Community
K. UNICEF
L. Salvation Army
M. Trócaire
N. St Vincent de Paul
O. Irish Society for the Prevention of Cruelty to Animals
P. Voice
Q. Irish Wildlife Trust
R. Lion's Club
S. Irish Society for the Prevention of Cruelty to Children

Exercise 9: Gandhi

We all have a responsibility to look out for the rights of others.

When we do this we are also protecting our own rights. Read the story below of one man, Gandhi, who campaigned for the rights of others. Then answer the questions that follow.

Mahatma Gandhi (1869–1948) was born in India and studied law in England. After working as a lawyer for a short time in India, he went to live in South Africa. He discovered that Indians were treated very badly there. So he began to campaign for their rights. Even though he was against violence of any kind and his protest was always peaceful, he was in prison many times. Eventually, because of his campaigns Indians were given some new rights.

When he returned from South Africa he became involved in India's struggle for independence from England. Again, he approved of only peaceful protest, such as asking people not to buy British goods and holding sit-down protests on the streets of India. Gandhi himself often used fasting as a method of protest. He hoped that such methods would show the English that using violence against his fellow Indians would not keep them down or break their spirit. Gandhi said, 'the trouble with an eye for an eye is that it leaves the whole world blind'. In 1947, as a result of all these actions, India became an independent country.

Another great campaign in Gandhi's life was against the caste system in India. A caste is a social level or class. Under this system a person is born into a specific caste and may never leave it. The lowest class was called the 'untouchables'. These people lived in terrible poverty. Again, his peaceful campaigns on behalf of the 'untouchables' had good results and the lives of many Indians were improved.

Gandhi continued his peaceful campaigns until he was assassinated by a Hindu fanatic in 1948.

1. Name **three** different campaigns that Gandhi was involved in.

   a) ______________________________

   b) ______________________________

   c) ______________________________

2. Name **three** different forms of protest that Gandhi used.

   a) ______________________________

   b) ______________________________

   c) ______________________________

3. What do you understand by Gandhi's words '**the trouble with an eye for an eye is that it makes the whole world blind**'?

   ____

   ____

   ____

4. Name the American civil rights leader who was inspired by Gandhi's methods of non-violent protest (see *Impact!* textbook).

   ____

   ____

5. Name another method of peaceful protest not mentioned in Gandhi's story.

   ____

   ____

Exercise 10: People for Peace

Alfred Nobel was born in Sweden in 1833. Nobel invented dynamite and later built many companies all over the world. In his will he asked that his fortune be used to give prizes to those who have done their best in areas like peace, medicine and literature.

The Nobel Peace Prize is awarded each year to individuals and organisations who work in the area of peace and human rights.

1. Draw a line to match the person, or the logo of the organisation, with the description of the work for which they won the Nobel Peace Prize.

This organisation won for their worldwide work for the protection of the rights of prisoners of conscience.

This man won for his campaign for civil rights in America.

This organisation won for their contribution to peace around the world, as peacekeepers and peace makers.

This woman won for her work with the poor around the world.

These men won for their work to end apartheid and bring peace to South Africa.

Exercise 11: What Does it Mean to be a Good Citizen?

Read what some students have said being a good citizen means.

1. What does being a good citizen mean to you? Write your answers in the speech bubbles below.

Exercise 12: Building Citizen Blocks

Written on the blocks are ways in which you could become an active citizen, and ways in which you would not be an active citizen.

1. Use **green** to colour all bricks that would help you become an active citizen.
2. Use **red** to colour all the bricks that would mean you are **not** an active citizen.

You join a club in your community

You decide it's too much trouble to return your library books

You decide to visit an elderly neighbour

You always look for 'Fair Trade' goods in the supermarket

You don't bother to vote in the student council election

You take part in a fun run for a local charity

You pass up on the chance to go to a fundraising event for 'Concern'

You join a political party

You get involved in an anti-racist campaign in school

You decide it's too much trouble to recycle stuff

You always leave the lights and T.V. on when you go out

You decide to show a new student 'round the school

You pass up the chance to become a member of the Junior Amnesty International group in school

You join the 'Clean up the Park' campaign in your area

You join the 'Green Committee' in school

You decide you won't register to vote when you are 18.

3. Choose four good citizenship actions from the wall above and rank them in order of importance (a) to (d) .

a) ____

b) ____

c) ____

d) ____

4. In the blank bricks add your own ideas on how to become an active citizen ot not.

Exercise 13: How Green are You?

Answer the quiz by putting a circle around Always, Sometimes or Never.

1. Do you take a shower instead of a bath?

   Always *Sometimes* *Never*

2. Do you recycle cans and bottles?

   Always *Sometimes* *Never*

3. Do you walk or cycle to school?

   Always *Sometimes* *Never*

4. Do you turn the tap off when washing your teeth?

   Always *Sometimes* *Never*

5. Do you turn off the lights/TV/CD player when you are the last in a room?

   Always *Sometimes* *Never*

6. Do you use recycled paper?

   Always *Sometimes* *Never*

7. Do you use litter bins?

Always *Sometimes* *Never*

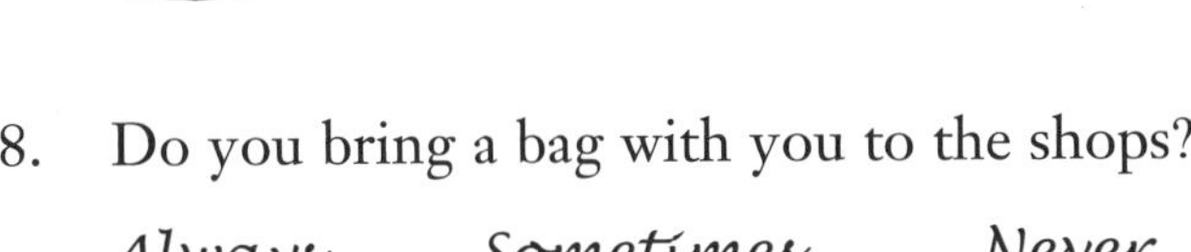

8. Do you bring a bag with you to the shops?

Always *Sometimes* *Never*

9. Do you only turn the washing machine on when it is full?

Always *Sometimes* *Never*

10. Do you use environmentally friendly deodorants?

Always *Sometimes* *Never*

Add up the number of times you have circled each to find out how green you are.

So How Green are You?

Mainly Always: Well, you are definitely green. Well done, and keep up the good work.

Score: __________

Mainly Sometimes: Getting green, but there is more you could do.

Score: __________

Mainly Never: You have a long way to go – start today.

Score: __________

Exercise 14: Don't Just Dump it!

One way to cut down on the amount of waste we produce is to:

Reduce - Reuse - Recycle - Repair

1. This dump contains many items that can be reused, recycled or repaired. Draw a line linking each item in the dump to the bin it belongs in.

2. Name **two** items not in the dump that could be reused, recycled or repaired.

   Item 1: ______________________

   Item 2: ______________________

3. How could you reduce the amount of water or electricity that you use?

____

____

____

Exercise 15: Green Energy

Coal, gas, oil and peat are the main sources of energy in Ireland. These are non-renewable sources of energy and will one day run out.

The blades of the windmill name sources of 'green energy'. Green energy is made from renewable energy sources.

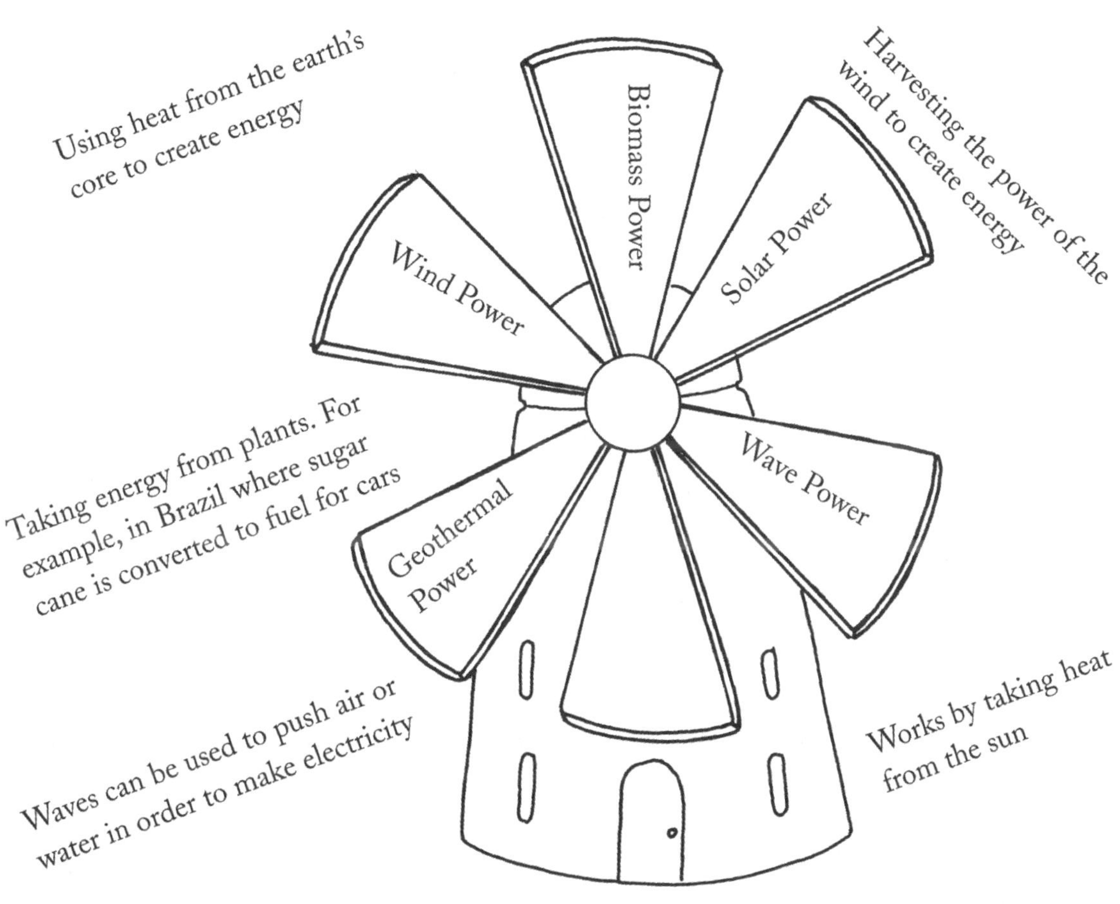

1. Use the 'green energy' sources from the windmill to complete the following sentences.

   a) *Energy made by taking heat from the sun is called* __________ __________.

   b) *We can take energy from plants, for example in Brazil sugar cane is made into fuel for cars. This kind of energy is called* __________ __________.

   c) *Waves can be used to push air or water to make electricity. This energy is* __________ __________.

   d) *Using the wind to create energy is called* __________ __________.

   e) *Using heat from the earth's core to make energy is called* __________ __________.

Exercise 16: The Green Car

As fossil fuels like oil – from which petrol is made – run out, other energy sources are being developed. Read the article below and answer the questions that follow.

Ford plan for UK car that runs on alcohol

Ford is to make the first serious attempt to bring alcohol-powered cars to Britain. Such vehicles are widespread in Sweden, where they make up 80 per cent of Ford Focus sales.

They have yet to take off in the UK, however, because garages don't sell the fuel.

Now Ford's launch of an alcohol-powered Focus for Britain next month will be coupled with a major drive to boost fuel outlets.

Next year, it will supply more than 100 alcohol-fired Focus models in Somerset to council officials, police and emergency services, as well as Wessex Water.

This will coincide with a scheme to create a network of alco-pumps in local filling stations. And Wessex Grain is to set up a factory in Somerset making alco-fuel from locally grown grain.

Alcohol for cars – known as bio-ethanol or 'bio-fuel' – is made from plants including sugar beet, grain and even wood. It produces half the carbon emissions of petrol – and, unlike oil, which eventually runs out of supply, producers can simply grow some more.

Cars need only slight modification to run on the 'green' fuel.

At a London conference yesterday, environmental groups were joined by Ford and Swedish car-maker Saab to call for Government help in providing pumps.

Campaigners say if bio-fuel replaced 5 per cent of petrol in the UK, it would be the pollution equivalent of taking a million cars off the road.

The fuel is simple to use. It is mixed with petrol and can be sold at garages with little need to alter pumps. Drivers notice no difference in vehicle performance.

Ray Massey, *Daily Mail*

1. In what country are alcohol powered cars widespread?

2. Why up to now have alcohol-powered cars not taken off in Britain?

3. According to this article what is Wessex Grain going to set up?

4. What is 'bio-fuel' made from?

5. Why is 'bio-fuel' a better choice for the environment than petrol?

6. According to campaigners, if bio-fuel replaced 5 per cent of petrol in the UK, what would it be the pollution equivalent of?

7. What arguments could be made to try and persuade car makers to start a scheme like this in Ireland?

Exercise 17: Rainforests

Tropical rainforests once covered over fourteen per cent of the earth's land; now rainforests cover less than six per cent. The rainforests are disappearing at the rate of eighty acres per minute. In the exercise below, match the reasons why some people want to continue to cut down the rainforests and others are against it. Draw a line matching the person to the reason.

'I need tropical hardwoods to sell the wood for furniture, house building and newspapers.'

'I need to clear the trees to make way for building houses and shopping centres.'

'I need to stop the cutting down of rainforests because the plants can be used for medical research.'

'The rainforests cannot be cut down as myself and my family will have nowhere to live.'

'The rainforests are needed to suck up all the CO_2 and pollutions.

'Stop cutting down the trees as my habitat will be destroyed and I will have nowhere to live.'

'I need to clear trees to make more places for cattle to grace.'

1. What do you think is the strongest reason for not cutting down the rainforests? Give two explanations for your answer.

   Reason: ______________________________

   Explanation 1: ______________________________

   ____

   Explanation 2: ______________________________

   ____

2. What two actions could you take to raise awareness about the importance of the rainforests?

   Action 1: ______________________________

   Action 2: ______________________________

3. Design a poster to show why the rainforests are important for everyone.

Exercise 18: Get the Picture!

Study this cartoon on environmental problems facing Ireland today and answer the questions that follow.

1. Looking through the window of this Minister's office can you name <u>two</u> causes of CO2 (carbon dioxide) pollution?

   a) ______________________________

   b) ______________________________

2. What is the Kyoto Agreement, trying to do?

   ____

   ____

3. Under the Kyoto Agreement, if Ireland does not cut down producing greenhouse gases what will happen?

   ____

   ____

4. What other greenhouses gas is mentioned in the report on the Minister's desk?

   ____

   ____

5. Where, according to the report, is this gas produced?

   ____

6. What three things in this Minister's office show concern about the environment?

   ____

   ____

7. What would you put on this Minister's 'To Do' list to help cut down on greenhouse gases and improve the environment in Ireland?

   ____

   ____

8. What CSPE concept can you come up with by adding six letters to this minister's first name?

   S ___ ___ ___ ___ ___ ___ SHIP

Exercise 19: Birthday Wishes

Imagine it is the earth's birthday today. It is 46 years old. This is its life story so far. Using the pictures below see if you can write the sections of the earth's life story that are missing. Sections 1 and 6 have been done already.

1. *Not much is known about the earth aged 0-41 years old.*

2. *At age 42 you can see on the earth ...*

____

____

____

____

____

____

3. *At age 43 you can see on the earth ...*

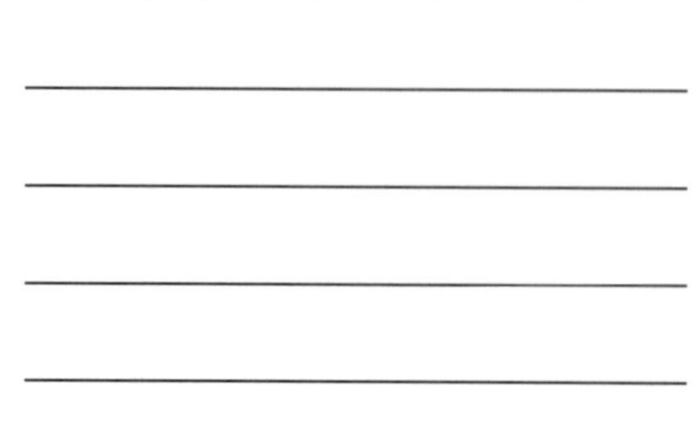

4. *At age 44 you can see on the earth ...*

____

____

____

____

____

____

5. *At age 45 you can see on the earth ...*

____

____

____

____

____

____

6. *In the last minute, just before the earth was 46 years old, human beings have caused the destruction of many hundreds of animals. We've used up many of the world's resources. We have weapons that can destroy the earth in seconds. All this has happened in the last minute of the world's imagined 46 years.*

Exercise 20: My Future

What will be
Left here for me
When I grow up?

Will there be
Pure air to breathe
Will the sea be clean?

Will tarmac
Cover all the fields
Will they still be green?

Milk from cows
Meat, veg and fruit
Will they be fit to eat?

Will sunlight hurt
Will fumes from cars
Clog up a crowded street?

Will blue whales sing
Will elephants
And rhinos still survive?

Will you have left
Us anything
Healthy and alive?

When I've grown up
And I'm in charge
What will it be worth
If you have used
The goodness up
And destroyed the Earth?

David Harmer

1. List three of the concerns that the author of this poem has about the future.

   a) ______________________________

   b) ______________________________

   c) ______________________________

2. What actions can you take to make sure that the future will not be as the author of this poem fears?

   Action 1: ______________________________

   Action 2: ______________________________

Exercise 21: My Pledge

What positive actions could you and your classmates take to help improve your school environment?

In the globe below name four actions that you will take in the next month that will improve your school environment, and explain how you will carry them out.

Example

Action: I will help cut down on the amount of electricity used in school.

Action plan: When leaving the classroom I will turn off the lights.

Exercise 22: Revision

Rights and Responsibilities Word Search

D	D	N	Y	R	H	Y	Y	Z	P	C	F	E	F	H
C	E	K	O	U	I	T	D	R	N	O	L	J	Q	O
R	E	C	M	I	S	G	O	X	E	N	C	L	Z	I
M	N	A	L	E	N	T	H	G	E	V	C	P	J	O
F	N	O	N	A	E	I	P	T	D	E	Y	A	L	P
P	X	M	E	C	R	X	P	L	S	N	L	A	G	R
H	A	J	T	E	K	A	W	O	Q	T	K	W	N	W
L	R	I	K	F	M	S	T	C	Y	I	E	F	Y	T
A	O	D	Z	H	Q	Y	B	I	X	O	S	N	I	C
N	L	A	V	I	V	R	U	S	O	N	N	Q	B	L
Q	P	T	G	V	F	M	H	H	J	N	O	L	I	R
D	Y	S	Y	C	S	R	O	Z	G	Z	I	H	G	O
V	O	H	F	Z	E	N	J	D	B	A	T	J	P	J
H	K	F	R	F	L	J	U	G	J	O	A	K	D	R
W	F	Q	U	N	I	T	E	D	V	A	N	H	G	M

Find these words in the grid above.

AMNESTY	RIGHTS	PLAY	NEEDS
HUMAN	CONVENTION	SURVIVAL	PROTECTION
OPINION	NATIONS	DECLARATION	UNITED

Word Grid

Use the clues below to fill in the word grid.

Across

1. This is when you have a view of a person or group before you meet them.
4. These go hand in hand with responsibilities.
5. When you put your bottles in the bottle bank you do this.
6. This group is concerned with rights around the world.
7. This is when two sides meet each other half-way.
9. When you bring a bag to the shops you do this.

Down

2. Every choice has one of these.
3. A group of people that are discriminated against in Irish society.
8. The United Nations wrote down a list of rights in this.

Word Grid

The Environment

Use the clues below to fill in the word grid.

Across

3. This energy is made by taking heat from the sun.
4. Another word for dump.
5. You can do this with glass bottles.
6. When you bring your own plastic bag to the shop you are doing this.

Down

1. These are non-renewable sources of energy.
2. You will find these in the Amazon, but they are disappearing fast.

Section 2

CSPE

Exercise 1: What's a Community?

1. In the circles below name the people you would meet in an average week who are members of these communities.

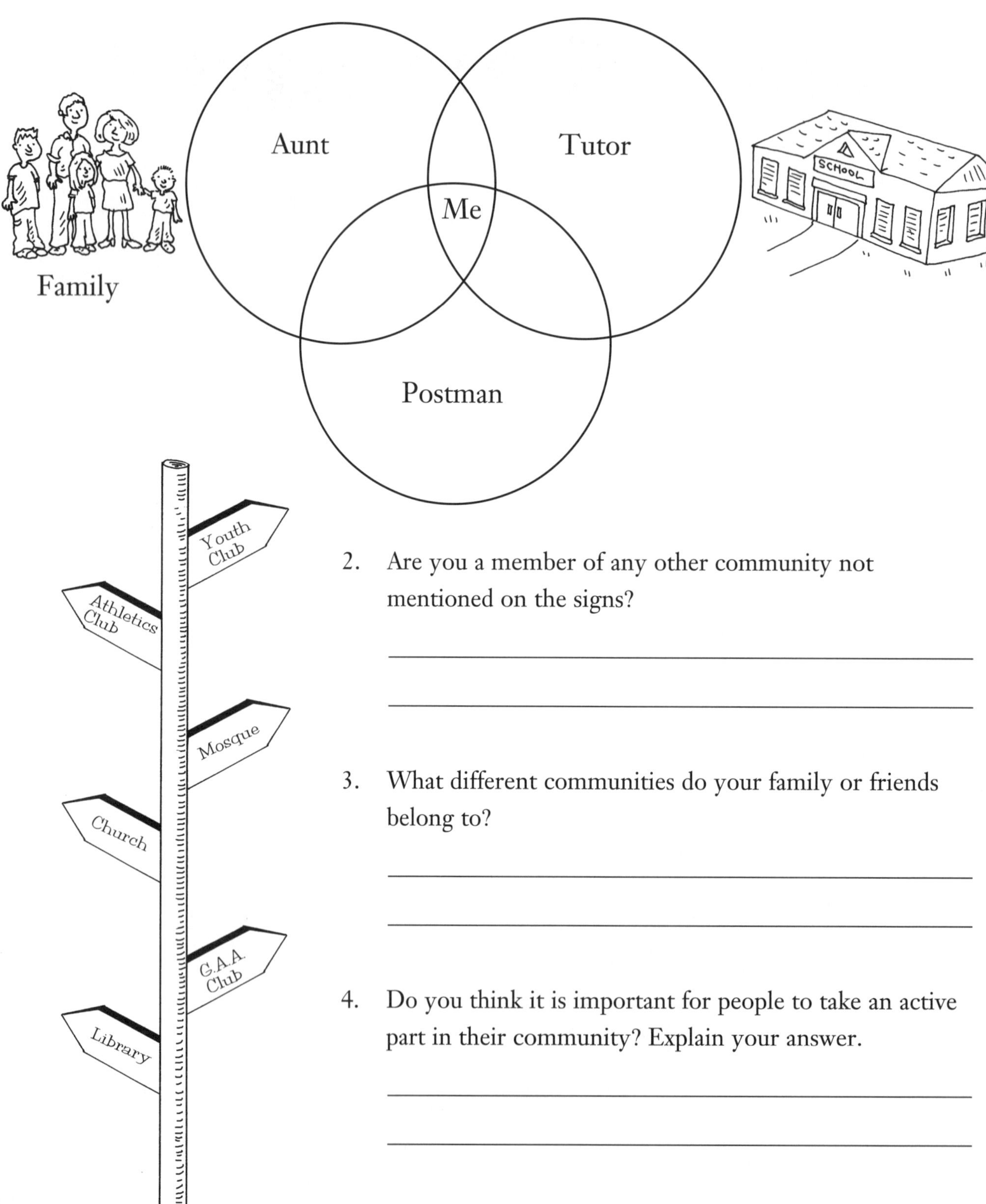

2. Are you a member of any other community not mentioned on the signs?

____

____

3. What different communities do your family or friends belong to?

____

____

4. Do you think it is important for people to take an active part in their community? Explain your answer.

____

____

Exercise 2: Councillor Dogood and Dreamsville

Each local authority is responsible for drawing up a development plan for its area. This is usually done every five years. A development plan normally covers such topics as the development of run-down areas, the improvement of parks and public areas, road improvements, preservation of historical buildings, and what sort of land should be used for housing, schools, factories and shops. Following approval by the county councillors the development plan is put on public display in places like libraries so that any person can make an objection to the plan if they wish.

1. Study this map of a town called Dreamsville and write a letter to Councillor Dogood, mentioning: a) any good points; b) any bad points; and c) any suggestions that you might have to make the proposed new town development better.

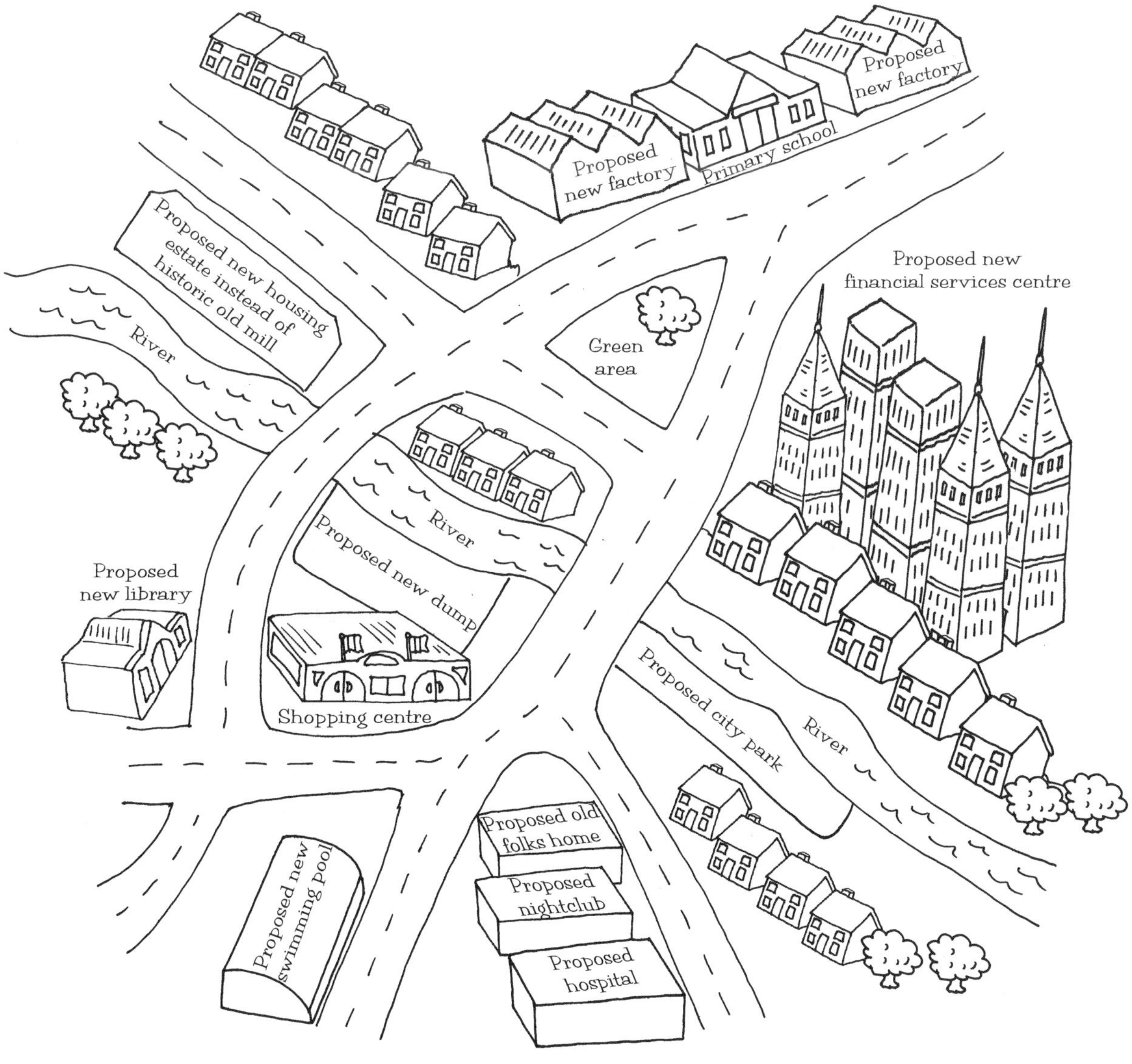

Proposed new factory
Proposed new factory
Primary school
Proposed new housing estate instead of historic old mill
River
Green area
Proposed new financial services centre
River
Proposed new dump
Proposed new library
Shopping centre
Proposed city park
River
Proposed new swimming pool
Proposed old folks home
Proposed nightclub
Proposed hospital

Councillor Dogood
Urban District Council
Dreamsville

Dear Councillor Dogood,

____

Yours sincerely,

Exercise 3: Making a Stand

Read the newspaper headlines below and answer the questions that follow.

LOCAL RESIDENTS TAKE TO AIRWAVES OVER POST OFFICE CLOSING

LOCAL ENVIRONMENTAL GROUP STAGE PROTEST OVER PLANNED INCINERATOR PLANT

PARENTS AND STUDENTS MARCH OVER STATE OF SCHOOL BUILDING

LOCAL HISTORICAL GROUP RAISES MONEY TO STOP DEMOLITION OF BUILDING

RESIDENTS PETITION COUNCIL FOR TRAFFIC-CALMING MEASURES

Save our Post Office

Stop the crazy traffic

No toxic waste

Save our town

POSTER CAMPAIGN FOR BETTER CANCER CARE FACILITIES NEEDED IN SOUTH EAST

1. Name six issues that these headlines are highlighting.

   a) ______________________________

   b) ______________________________

   c) ______________________________

   d) ______________________________

   e) ______________________________

   f) ______________________________

2. Name six ways in which these community groups took action over the issues of concern to them.

   a) ______________________________

   b) ______________________________

   c) ______________________________

   d) ______________________________

   e) ______________________________

   f) ______________________________

3. Name one local issue that concerns you and suggest a form of action that you could take over the issue.

   Issue: ______________________________

   ____

   ____

   ____

   Action: ______________________________

   ____

   ____

   ____

   ____

   ____

Exercise 4: Save the Woods

Green areas around towns and cities are very important. Many people like to walk in the countryside and enjoy the fresh air. Read the following story of what happened when a forest was in danger of being sold off, and answer the questions that follow.

Campaign to Save Woods

A campaign to save Togher Woods has been established by two local men in the wake of the news that the popular forest area is in danger of being sold off for use as a motor racing park.

The campaign received a major boost when Ian Lumley, Heritage Officer at An Taisce* contacted the group to lend their support. Since news broke on Tuesday of last week that the 300-acre Coillte** forest at Togher is in danger of being sold off for commercial development the campaign wasted no time in getting up and running.

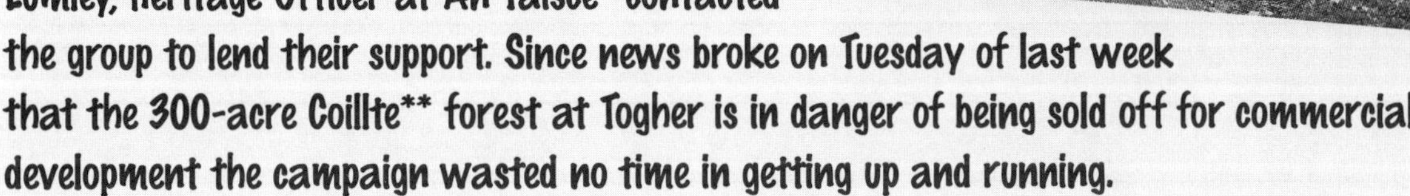

Denis Donoghue and Eamon Donovan, the campaign organisers, had a website up and running with 48 hours of the private meeting between the developer and Portlaoise Town Council on Tuesday.

The website, which can be accessed on www.savetogherwood.com, gives the campaign the opportunity to reach a very wide audience throughout Laois, Ireland and even abroad.

A petition to save the wood has also been circulated to shops around Portlaoise and the petition can also be signed online.

Laois Nationalist

1. Why did the campaign to save Togher Woods start? ______________________________

____

____

____

*An Taisce is an organisation that campaigns for a better environment.
**Coillte is a company that manages Ireland's forests.

2. How did the campaign receive a major boost? ____________________

3. What did the campaign organisers get up and running?

4. How could this be very helpful in their campaign?

5. What else has been organised as part of the campaign?

6. What other actions could you suggest that would raise awareness about this campaign?

Exercise 5: Good Developments

Developments in communities do not always have to cause problems. Read the following story about an idea that the Mayor of Paris had and answer the questions that follow.

In 2002 the Socialist Mayor of Paris came up with the idea to turn 3 km on the right bank of the River Seine, smack in the middle of Paris, into a beach. The man-made beach beside the river comes with white sand, palm trees, sunbeds and parasols.

As well as enjoying the beach visitors can enjoy the following: picnic tables, Tai Chi, beach volleyball, a climbing wall, a floating stage, book lending library booths, bicycle rental facilities, as well as concerts, music and dancing.

Three thousand tonnes of fine sand are used to cover the area and families who cannot leave the city for holidays have a chance to pretend they are at the seaside. Many families bring picnics and chill out for the day.

As the River Seine is not suitable for swimming, in 2004 a 28-metre pool was added so people could have somewhere to cool off in the heat of the summer sun.

All this, however, does not come cheap and it costs over €2 million to run. Most of the money comes from business sponsors, and it is a huge hit with the people of Paris.

It now attracts about 3 million visitors every year between July and August, the period of time for which it is open.

1. What idea did the mayor of Paris come up with?

2. Besides relaxing on the beach, what else is in place for the people of Paris to enjoy?

3. How is the project paid for?

4. How many visitors does it attract every summer?

5. Can you think of any ideas like this one that would make the town or city you live in more fun in the summertime?

6. If you came up with a good idea, who would you contact who might help your dream of a better town or city come true? Explain the reason for your choice.

Exercise 6: Community Alert

The Gardaí rely on the public to report crimes, to act as good citizens and to help them in their work. Community Alert is one project in which the community works with the Gardaí.

What is Community Alert?

A project organised by voluntary community groups with the Gardaí and aimed at preventing attacks on people in rural areas, especially the elderly.

Community Alert has three main objectives

1. Taking steps to show the elderly that the community cares for them.
2. Giving the elderly advice on how to protect themselves from attack and robbery.
3. Encouraging the elderly to report to the Gardaí any person behaving suspiciously around their house or in the area.

Read the brochure and answer the questions that follow.

1. Name **TWO** organisations that are supporting the Garda Síochána's Community Alert project.

   Name of the first organisation: ______________________________

   Name of the second organisation: ______________________________

2. Which particular group of people in the community is this project trying to protect?

___

3. Why does this particular group of people need help and advice from projects like the Community Alert project? Give **THREE** reasons.

   First reason: ___

   ___

   Second reason: ___

   ___

   Third reason: ___

   ___

4. Name **ONE** other group that the Garda Síochána help in the community and describe **TWO** ways they help this group.

   Name of the group: ___

   ___

   How the Gardaí help them: ___

   ___

   How the Gardaí help them: ___

   ___

5. Describe in detail **ONE** way in which a group of school students could help elderly people living in their community.

   ___

   ___

   ___

(Questions from D.E.S. exam paper.)

Exercise 7: Vote for Me

Imagine that you are a candidate in a local election. Fill out this election manifesto saying what you will do for your area if you are elected. Keep in mind that local authorities are responsible for certain programmes. (See an explanation of these areas in your *Impact!* textbook, page 59.) Think about what your area needs most.

In the manifesto say whether you are running as an independent candidate or with a political party.

Party Logo:

Name: ______________________________

Campaign slogan: ______________________________

____

If I am elected I will ...

____

____

____

____

____

____

____

____

____

____

Hints:

- *What about your parks and public areas? Are they in good condition?*
- *Do you have enough recycling depots?*
- *Do you have a swimming pool?*
- *What about traffic and parking?*
- *Are roads in your area in good condition?*
- *Are there enough places for young people to go, enough things for people to do?*
- *Do you have an athletic track?*
- *Do you have a Tidy Towns Committee?*
- *Should your town be a 'Fair Trade' town?*

Exercise 8: Revision

Your Community Word Search

Y	A	A	O	B	C	O	S	L	O	N	D	N	S	C
T	W	M	X	I	X	T	Y	A	Z	T	T	N	J	O
I	N	E	I	G	H	B	O	U	R	H	O	O	D	U
R	P	R	O	X	N	J	M	E	U	I	L	Y	M	N
O	K	L	P	Q	J	O	S	T	T	B	B	R	U	C
H	I	T	A	W	A	I	I	C	X	N	G	A	A	I
T	T	R	E	Y	D	J	E	T	N	E	N	R	C	L
U	M	I	G	E	G	L	V	W	I	N	W	B	M	L
A	M	J	N	E	E	R	L	Q	Q	T	A	I	G	O
L	W	T	T	L	G	U	O	K	N	H	E	L	V	R
A	S	O	A	B	N	J	I	U	L	Y	R	P	W	R
C	V	C	Y	B	Y	C	Z	L	N	U	V	F	N	L
O	O	N	G	I	A	P	M	A	C	D	N	J	O	D
L	I	N	P	V	F	J	U	A	K	T	S	D	W	G
D	H	N	E	X	S	R	Z	E	B	I	H	P	V	A

Find these words in the grid above.

CAMPAIGN	LOCAL ELECTIONS
LOCAL AUTHORITY	PLAYGROUNDS
PETITION	LIBRARY
VOTE	NEIGHBOURHOOD
COUNCILLOR	RESIDENTS

Word Grid

Use the clues below to fill in the word grid.

Across

1. Every building needs this kind of permission.
3. We are all members of this.
6. A kind of action.
7. You elect these to your area.

Down

2. The President's Award.
4. A county could have this.
5. You do this when you decide what land should be used for what purpose.

Take Action Word Search

L	G	N	M	B	N	T	S	R	S	B	G	Q	S	X
B	E	D	O	S	U	R	V	E	Y	U	H	U	T	Y
W	G	T	R	I	E	R	N	E	E	K	K	E	E	S
Q	J	P	T	T	T	A	F	S	I	E	N	S	L	I
D	K	D	S	E	W	I	T	P	A	K	T	T	F	E
Q	N	O	Z	I	R	S	T	C	O	S	S	I	A	N
C	P	X	V	G	P	W	X	E	W	C	F	O	E	X
H	V	O	P	E	I	Q	R	K	P	J	G	N	L	E
Y	M	A	A	Y	U	W	G	I	J	O	P	N	I	K
Q	G	K	E	Y	H	S	N	U	T	C	H	A	J	U
F	E	S	Z	F	D	P	R	L	X	I	B	I	B	G
R	V	R	L	O	P	O	P	A	W	Z	N	R	S	R
A	G	N	I	S	I	A	R	D	N	U	F	E	H	X
D	Y	Z	R	P	K	D	U	Q	J	D	I	U	V	I
B	P	Q	N	Z	S	V	Y	C	K	X	H	R	I	S

Find these words in the grid above.

FUNDRAISING	POSTERS
GUEST SPEAKER	QUESTIONNAIRE
LEAFLETS	SURVEY
PETITION	

Section 3

CSPE

Exercise 1: Democracy at Work

The following leaflet describes democracy at work. Read the leaflet and answer the questions.

Ireland's democracy is based on the Constitution.
Achtaíodh an Bunreacht sa bhliain 1937.

In a general election all Irish people over the age of 18 have a say (a vote) on deciding how they want the country run.
I gcóras daonlathach, is iad an pobal a chinneann cé hiad na daoine ar mian leo iad a bheith i mbun na tíre.

At Dáil Éireann in Leinster House, the TDs elected to represent the people debate new laws (called Bills) and make changes to existing laws.
Sa Dáil, bíonn díospóireacht ag Teachtaí Dála i dtaobh Billí agus féadfaidh siad an Rialtas a cheistiú faoin tslí a bhfuil an tír á rith acu.

The Seanad works with the Dáil in the development of the country's laws.
Le bheith ceadaithe sa Dáil agus sa Seanad araon, ní mór tacaíocht níos mó ná a leath (tromlach) de na comhaltaí a bheith le Billí.

Parliamentary Committees are set up to debate Bills on behalf of the Dáil or the Seanad. This helps to speed up difficult work.
Coistí Oireachtais a dhéanann cuid d'obair na Dála agus an tSeanaid, agus is tábhachtaí ná riamh an chuid sin den obair.

The President signs a Bill into law when it has been passed by the Dáil and the Seanad.
Nuair a chuireann an tUachtarán a lámh le Bille, is dlí é.

The Bills passed through the Oireachtas (the President, the Dáil, the Seanad) help make Ireland a safe and fair place for all people to live in.
Is trí na ranna éagsúla rialtais a chuirtear na Billí a ritear san Oireachtas i ngníomh.

Democracy at work

TITHE AN OIREACHTAIS

HOUSES OF THE OIREACHTAS

1. Circle the following words in the 'Democracy at Work' leaflet.
   - Constitution
   - Seanad
   - General Election
   - TDs
   - Laws
   - President
   - Bill
   - Committee
   - Parliamentary
   - Oireachtas
   - Dáil Éireann
   - Democracy

2. Choose six of the words you have circled and use each in a sentence to explain what it means.

   a) ______________________________

   b) ______________________________

   c) ______________________________

   d) ______________________________

   e) ______________________________

   f) ______________________________

3. Underline or circle in *red* what age you have to be to vote.

4. Underline or circle in *blue* what TDs do in the Dáil.

5. Underline or circle in *black* what happens at Parliamentary committees.

6. Underline or circle in *green* how a bill is signed into law.

Exercise 2: Ballot Paper

1. Fill out the sample ballot paper below in order of your first, second, third, fourth, etc. choices.
2. Name a TD who is an Independent.

   ____

3. How many candidates on this ballot paper are Independent candidates? ____________
4. Which political party has the most number of candidates?

   ____

5. What **three** pieces of information are included about each candidate on the ballot paper?

   a) ____

   b) ____

   c) ____

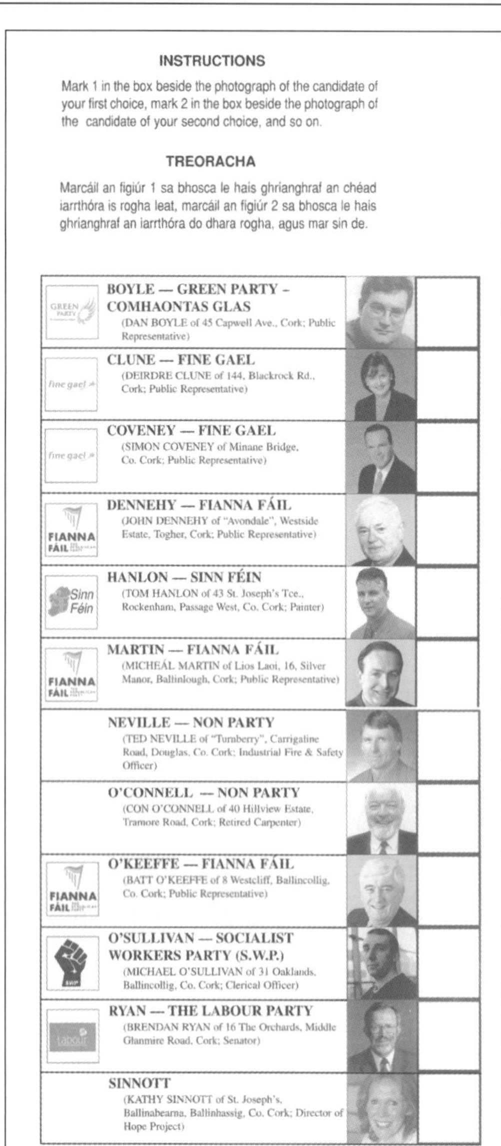

INSTRUCTIONS

Mark 1 in the box beside the photograph of the candidate of your first choice, mark 2 in the box beside the photograph of the candidate of your second choice, and so on.

TREORACHA

Marcáil an figiúr 1 sa bhosca le hais ghrianghraf an chéad iarrthóra is rogha leat, marcáil an figiúr 2 sa bhosca le hais ghrianghraf an iarrthóra do dhara rogha, agus mar sin de.

GREEN PARTY	**BOYLE — GREEN PARTY - COMHAONTAS GLAS** (DAN BOYLE of 45 Capwell Ave., Cork; Public Representative)		
fine gael	**CLUNE — FINE GAEL** (DEIRDRE CLUNE of 144, Blackrock Rd., Cork; Public Representative)		
fine gael	**COVENEY — FINE GAEL** (SIMON COVENEY of Minane Bridge, Co. Cork; Public Representative)		
FIANNA FÁIL	**DENNEHY — FIANNA FÁIL** (JOHN DENNEHY of "Avondale", Westside Estate, Togher, Cork; Public Representative)		
Sinn Féin	**HANLON — SINN FÉIN** (TOM HANLON of 43 St. Joseph's Tce., Rockenham, Passage West, Co. Cork; Painter)		
FIANNA FÁIL	**MARTIN — FIANNA FÁIL** (MICHEÁL MARTIN of Lios Laoi, 16, Silver Manor, Ballinlough, Cork; Public Representative)		
	NEVILLE — NON PARTY (TED NEVILLE of "Turnberry", Carrigaline Road, Douglas, Co. Cork; Industrial Fire & Safety Officer)		
	O'CONNELL — NON PARTY (CON O'CONNELL of 40 Hillview Estate, Tramore Road, Cork; Retired Carpenter)		
FIANNA FÁIL	**O'KEEFFE — FIANNA FÁIL** (BATT O'KEEFFE of 8 Westcliff, Ballincollig, Co. Cork; Public Representative)		
SWP	**O'SULLIVAN — SOCIALIST WORKERS PARTY (S.W.P.)** (MICHAEL O'SULLIVAN of 31 Oaklands, Ballincollig, Co. Cork; Clerical Officer)		
Labour	**RYAN — THE LABOUR PARTY** (BRENDAN RYAN of 16 The Orchards, Middle Glanmire Road, Cork; Senator)		
	SINNOTT (KATHY SINNOTT of St. Joseph's, Ballinabearna, Ballinhassig, Co. Cork; Director of Hope Project)		

Exercise 3: At The Table

Look at this cabinet meeting. Can you identify from the list below which minister would say what? Draw a line to connect each minister with the most appropriate statement.

1.	Minister for Education and Science	A.	*'I think we should increase unemployment benefit.'*
2.	Minister for Finance	B.	*'I want more money for schools.'*
3.	Minister for Communications, Marine and Natural Resources	C.	*'We need to be careful that there isn't another outbreak of Foot and Mouth.'*
4.	Minister for Community, Rural and Gaeltacht Affairs	D.	*'I want to introduce stiffer sentences for joy-riders.'*
5.	Minister for Transport	E.	*'I want to expand the Air Corps and Naval Service.'*
6.	Minister for the Environment and Local Government	F.	*'I'm concerned about the number of tourists coming to Ireland.'*
7.	Minister for Foreign Affairs	G.	*'I'm hoping to visit some Irish embassies abroad.'*
8.	Minister for Defence	H.	*'I want more money to create jobs.'*
9.	Minister for Agriculture and Food	I.	*'I want more laws made to control pollution.'*
10.	Minister for Justice, Equality and Law Reform	J.	*'What about more support for Irish-speaking areas?'*
11.	Minister for Health and Children	K.	*'I want to introduce higher taxes in the next budget.'*
12.	Minister for Social and Family Affairs	L.	*'I want to improve our hospital services.'*
13.	Minister for Enterprise, Trade and Employment	M.	*'Is anyone here concerned about new EU fishing policies?'*
14.	Minister for Arts, Sport and Tourism	N.	*'We need to put more money into the railways.'*

Exercise 4: Government of Ireland Quiz

Circle the correct answers to see how much you know about how Ireland is governed.

1. In Ireland the type of government we have is called:

   Dictatorship *Democracy* *Communism*

2. Democracy is government of people:

   By one person *By a king or queen* *By all the people*

3. The parliament in Ireland is called:

   Reichstag *Dáil* *Senate*

4. A person becomes a member of the Dáil by:

   Applying by letter *Being asked by the president* *Being elected*

5. Members of the Dáil are called:

   Ministers *TDs* *MEPs*

6. The head of the government is called:

   Prime Minister *President* *Taoiseach*

7. How many TDs sit in the national parliament?

   150 *166* *70*

8. The main job of government is to:

   Run the civil service *Build new transport systems* *Make new laws*

9. How many constituencies is Ireland divided into?

   110 *42* *56*

10. Who is the commander-in-chief of the Armed Forces?

    Taoiseach *Tánaiste* *President*

11. The Seanad is made up of:

60 senators   45 senators   95 senators

12. The civil service changes when a new government comes in:

Always   Sometimes   Never

13. The number of ministers in any government is set by the constitution at no more than:

5 ministers   10 ministers   15 ministers

14. Which type of government do we have in Ireland now?

Majority   Minority   Coalition

15. Whose job is it to appoint ministers to a government?

President   Taoiseach   Civil Service

16. What is the highest court in Ireland?

Circuit Court   Special Criminal Court   Supreme Court

17. In order to vote in an election you must be aged at least:

17   18   25

18. A presidential election must be held every:

4 years   5 years   7 years

19. A general election must be held every:

4 years   5 years   7 years

20. The constitution can only be changed by:

The government   A referendum   A general election

Check Chapter 3 in your *Impact!* textbook to see how well you did.

Total Score: $\frac{\quad}{20}$

Exercise 5: What does Ireland need?

Look at the statements made by these people. What issues do they think are important?

'I think we have to do more about joy-riding.'

'I think that we need better transport in our cities.'

'I think that we need to do more to protect our environment.'

'I think we need to spend more money building up our army and defence forces.'

'I think that young people should do more voluntary work.'

1. Name the **five** issues that these students are concerned with.

   a) ____________________

   b) ____________________

   c) ____________________

   d) ____________________

   e) ____________________

2. Name **two** other issues and say why you think they are of national importance.

   Issue: ____________________

   Why you think it is important: ____________________

   ____

   Issue: ____________________

   Why you think it is important: ____________________

   ____

3. Imagine that you are living in a country in the developing world. Write down a list of issues that you think would be important in your life.

   ____

   ____

4. Do you tthink that issues facing people in Ireland are different from issues facing people in the developing world? Explain your answer.

   ____

   ____

Exercise 6: Ciara's Story

The Simon Community is one organisation in Ireland that works with people who are homeless. The Simon Community estimates that about 10,000 people experience homelessness each year. Simon sees homelessness as more than being without a roof or house. It is about lack of shelter, lack of security, lack of belonging and lack of safety.

Read this story about Ciara, a 19-year-old teenager, and her experience of being without a home.

A Day in the Life of a Homeless Teenager: Ciara's Story

I feel a dull throbbing in my right leg. Slowly awakening from a restless night, I come around. Looking up, I notice a man pulling his hobnailed boot away from my lower leg. As he aims again, I quickly but painfully move my body. He looks, laughs, and walks on. As I try to get up, an old lady approaches. She smiles at me in a sympathetic way, but I think she just wants to make herself feel better about passing me by.

It is 12 o'clock and I'm hungry. I still feel tired because each time I closed my eyes last night I was terrified of getting a kick from everyone who passed by. Now I am both tired and hungry. I would love somewhere warm to sit and eat. I suddenly remember the three pounds that a drunken passer-by threw at me last night. Oh how I'd love a burger – my heart warms at the thought – but then I remember the last time I went to a chipper. The looks I got on the way in, you'd swear I was an axe murderer – looks of disgust, horror, embarrassment, and one of sheer terror. I'm only a girl of 19 and I definitely amn't big, so I can't understand why I frighten people so much. Anyway, the big security guard came that day and asked me to leave.

When I told him all wanted was a burger, he caught me by the neck and dragged me out the door. I wanted to die, but couldn't 'cos the last time I tried the ambulance came and I ended up in a strange hospital with a strange nurse looking down at me.

So today I have to go down to what I'm told is a 'social welfare officer'. I've been there before. The woman down there seemed nice at the beginning, but said I couldn't get any money until I had a place to stay. But when I went looking for a place to stay, I was told I needed money for rent first. Now I know I didn't finish my Leaving Cert, but I'm not sure anybody could figure this one out.

All want is somewhere to sit down and talk to somebody – is this too much to ask for? I've tried the library, but they kicked me out too. I feel a bit sick from thinking about all this, so I go to the doctor. But when I go in the door that says 'doctor's surgery', I'm told I need a medical card, which I don't have.

I stumble back out again – still cold, still hungry, still confused, and still not knowing what to do. I realise the only place I can get company and some comfort is the park. There I know I will end up drinking and out of control, but that's all that makes me feel good about myself. On reaching the park, I meet Tom, an elderly but friendly homeless person who treats me like I'm someone special. He offers me a drink and I am glad to have it. After a couple of drinks, I become sad with myself and tell Tom how depressed I am. He says something about Simon – I wonder who Simon is. Tom takes me to a shelter where I meet the first friendly stranger in days. They open the gate and let me in. I am taken to a small but comfortable room where I sit down and am asked nicely about myself and my history. They offer me a bed, a warm meal, and a shower and reassure me that they will help me look after my money and medical card and any other things I need. For the first time in nearly six months, I feel safe.

Extract from Simon Community Educational Pack

Questions about Ciara's story:

1. Why does Ciara not want to go to the chipper?

____

____

2. What does Ciara need to have in order to get social welfare money?

____

____

3. Where does Ciara sometimes go to rest?

4. When Ciara goes to Simon what is she offered?

5. What rights do you think Ciara is being denied?

6. Besides organisations like Simon Community, who else do you think is responsible for caring for people who are homeless?

7. What other organisations look out for the rights of people who are homeless?

Exercise 7: Getting the Picture

Read the information on the posters and answer the questions.

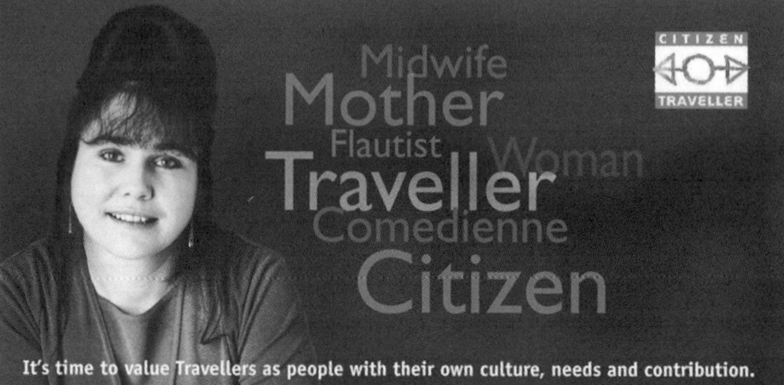

1. What does the poster of the man tell us about him?

____

____

2. What does the poster of the woman tell us about her?

____

____

3. What does the poster of the child tell us about her?

____

____

4. Why do you think so many words are used in each poster?

____

____

5. Do you think that this is a good campaign to show that Travellers make a positive contribution to Irish society? Give reasons for your answer.

____

____

____

Exercise 8: Advertise it!

Imagine that you work for an advertising agency. You have been hired by a group in Irish society that does not feel they have been treated equally. The group wants you to produce a poster.

This group wants to have a positive image to use in their campaign to show why they should be treated equally. They want the campaign to show that they make a positive contribution to Irish society. They do not want to be pitied by anyone.

Name the group that you are working for and design your poster in the box below.

Name of group: ___________________________________

(Exercise adapted from *All Different All Equal*, National Youth Council of Ireland.)

Exercise 9: Building Your Campaign

Written on the bricks below are some of the ways a campaign could be helped or hindered.

1. Use *green* to colour thc bricks that would help you in your campaign.
2. Use *red* to colour the bricks that would not help your campaign.

You organise a committee to help with the campaign.

The different people on the committee can't work together.

You contact other groups asking for their support.

Your request for a meeting with a government minister was turned down.

You don't have enough people to distribute the leaflets and do the questionnaire.

You put together information leaflets on the issue.

Your friends and family join the campaign.

A newspaper reporter tells you that he is not interested in writing an article about your issue.

TDs and councillors do not support your campaign.

You don't know where to go to find out more about the issue.

You don't feel confident enough to give interviews on the issue.

You know how to use the internet to get information.

You don't really believe you can bring about change.

A local business gives money to your cause.

You gather other views on the issue by carrying out a questionnaire.

You give a radio interview on your issue.

A newspaper agrees to highlight your issue.

You have a lot of responsibilities and don't have time to run the campaign.

You raise the issue with TDs and councillors.

You have a strong belief that you can bring about change.

You don't have enough money to run the campaign.

3. Choose **five** ways in which a campaign can be made successful. Rank them in order of importance.

a) ______________________________

b) ______________________________

c) ______________________________

d) ______________________________

e) ______________________________

Exercise 10: Equality and the Law

Under the Employment Equality Acts (1998 and 2004) and the Equal Status Acts (2000 and 2004) you cannot discriminate against a person on the following grounds:

- *race*
- *gender*
- *disability*
- *religion*
- *family status*
- *marital status*
- *being a member of the Travelling Community*
- *sexual orientation*
- *age.*

1. In the spaces below each picture say on what grounds the person is being discriminated against. Hint: look at the nine grounds above.

a) This person is being discriminated against on the grounds of

____________________.

b) This person is being discriminated against on the grounds of

____________________.

c) This person is being discriminated against on the grounds of

____________________.

d) This person is being discriminated against on the grounds of

____________________.

2. Fill in the blanks:

_ _ S _ _ _ _ _ _ _ _ _ _ _ _ _ means treating someone less favourably than you would treat another person. In the above cases, you would be breaking the _ A _.

Exercise 11: Crime Stop

Crimestoppers is an organisation that works with the Gardaí and the community to help solve crime. Study the poster and answer the questions about it.

1. What THREE points have Crimestoppers put on their poster to encourage people to phone them?

   First point ______________________________

   Second point ______________________________

   Third point ______________________________

2. Name ONE business company or organisation that is supporting this campaign.

   ____

3. Describe TWO actions that a local community could take to try and stop crime in their area. *These actions must not break the law.*

   First action: ______________________________

   ____

   ____

   ____

   Second action: ______________________________

   ____

   ____

   ____

4. Suggest TWO reasons why it might be difficult for a young person like yourself to report crime.

   First reason: ______________________________

   ____

   ____

   ____

   Second reason: ______________________________

   ____

   ____

   ____

(Taken from the Junior Certificate examination 2000, Department of Education and Science.)

Exercise 12: Revision

Voting Word Search

Z	L	H	B	K	D	F	D	Y	H	R	H	D	E	R
N	O	I	T	A	T	S	G	N	I	L	L	O	P	E
B	C	F	Q	O	O	F	H	M	Y	I	P	O	T	P
Q	V	H	L	B	O	U	Z	C	Z	N	L	N	Q	A
L	T	X	R	O	R	B	A	O	V	I	A	V	H	P
K	W	J	T	V	D	R	G	F	U	L	K	G	B	T
L	C	F	E	J	C	S	L	N	P	E	K	H	U	O
E	S	P	U	O	F	C	M	V	I	H	M	I	G	L
E	L	P	M	C	W	V	J	U	F	L	W	D	E	L
L	I	E	X	Y	C	R	A	W	K	O	L	B	I	A
Q	D	W	C	A	O	D	S	W	K	S	X	O	E	B
U	A	D	V	T	W	A	K	K	C	K	D	E	P	P
O	B	Z	F	V	I	Z	W	D	V	X	C	Q	H	B
T	L	O	P	Z	I	O	R	E	G	I	S	T	E	R
A	A	M	B	E	M	B	N	P	I	G	K	R	R	N

Find these words in the grid above.

BALLOT PAPER
DEMOCRACY
ELECTION
POLLING BOOTH
POLLING STATION
QUOTA
REGISTER

Election Quiz

These are the steps to voting in an election. They are mixed up. Put them in the right order by using the table below.

A. Bring your polling card

B. Put your name on the Register of Electors

C. Go to the polling station

D. Fill in your ballot paper

E. Go to a polling booth

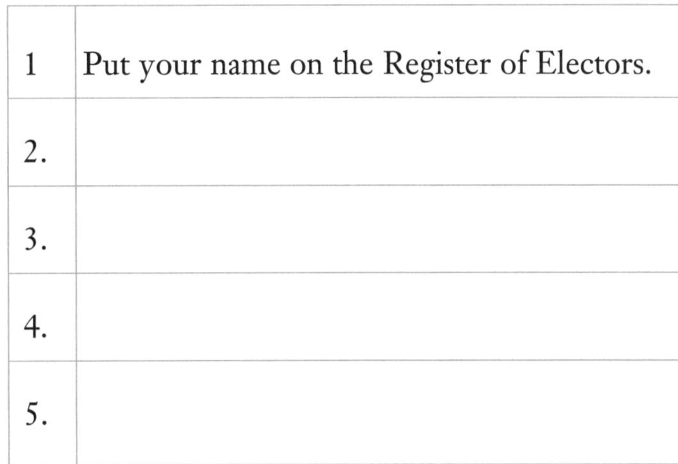

1	Put your name on the Register of Electors.
2.	
3.	
4.	
5.	

Check out your *Impact!* textbook to see if you've got it right!

Government Word Search

N	B	T	N	G	Q	A	V	E	H	S	E	Q	U	D
P	O	I	H	Z	B	U	D	C	B	T	S	K	G	K
N	K	I	D	E	J	F	A	B	O	H	U	K	J	R
M	L	D	T	K	S	E	Q	D	R	E	O	U	L	A
G	R	M	H	C	S	E	U	I	X	D	H	C	K	W
M	B	Q	W	I	E	M	A	D	H	A	R	I	C	O
I	Q	B	O	B	B	L	F	N	J	I	E	K	P	Y
J	G	A	R	C	E	C	E	J	A	L	T	P	G	N
N	T	D	R	C	N	M	F	L	W	D	S	R	B	M
G	Z	Y	L	W	V	Q	V	K	A	N	N	B	A	T
R	S	U	O	D	A	Z	U	J	V	R	I	H	U	Q
I	M	I	N	I	S	T	E	R	S	L	E	A	J	X
W	A	L	V	T	V	K	P	S	L	D	L	N	S	X
G	N	B	V	Z	E	R	J	S	J	G	J	Z	E	R
Z	I	Y	R	N	D	E	E	U	G	F	A	O	L	G

Find these words in this grid.

BILLS
GENERAL ELECTION
LAW
LEINSTER HOUSE
MINISTERS
TAOISEACH
THE DAIL
THE SEANAD

Government Word Search

Across

1. This is a government that is made up of two or more parties.
2. 166 TDs meet here.
3. What you are called if you stand for election.
4. Ministers are in charge of these.
5. Everyone over eighteen has the right to do this.
6. One of the houses of the Oireachtas.
7. You go out and vote in one of these.
8. The sorting of votes happens here.

Down

1. This contains the basic laws of our country.
2. A kind of party you could join.
3. A person needs to reach this before they can be elected.
4. Government of the people by the people.
5. A person who is not a member of a political party.

Section 4

CSPE

Exercise 1: The EU

Below is a map of the twenty-five EU countries.

1. Fill in the capitals of the countries that are missing from this map.
2. Which country in the centre of Europe is not a member of the EU?

   ____

3. Which Scandinavian country is not a member of the EU?

   ____

4. Which two European countries are likely to become members of the EU in 2007?

   a) ____

   b) ____

5. Here is a profile of the ten countries that joined the EU in May 2004; and of Bulgaria and Romania, which will join the EU in 2007. Fill in the name of the country on each flag below.

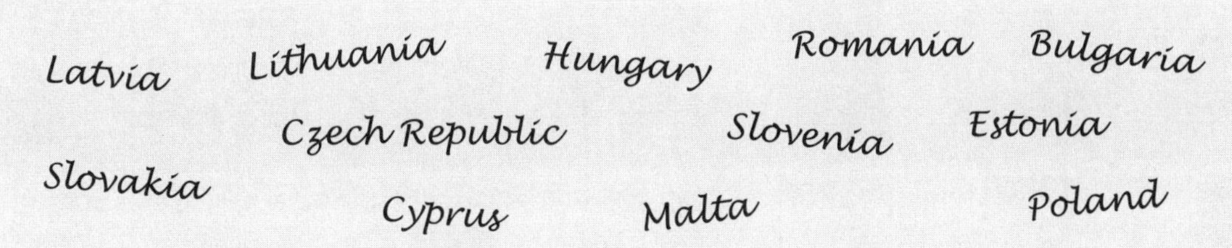

______
Population: 3.7 million citizens
Capital City: Vilnius
Land Area: 65,200 sq km
Languages: Lithuanian (Polish,Russian)

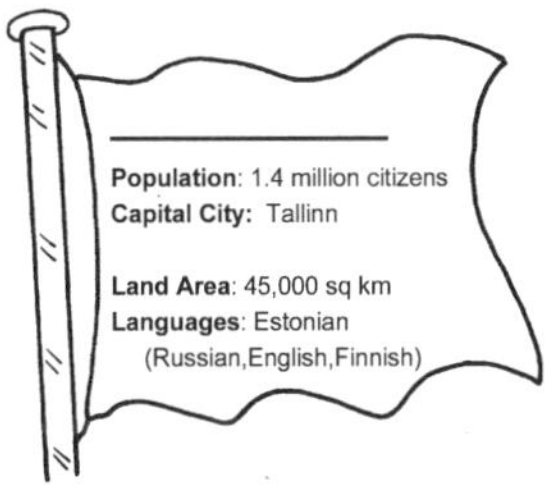

______
Population: 1.4 million citizens
Capital City: Tallinn
Land Area: 45,000 sq km
Languages: Estonian (Russian,English,Finnish)

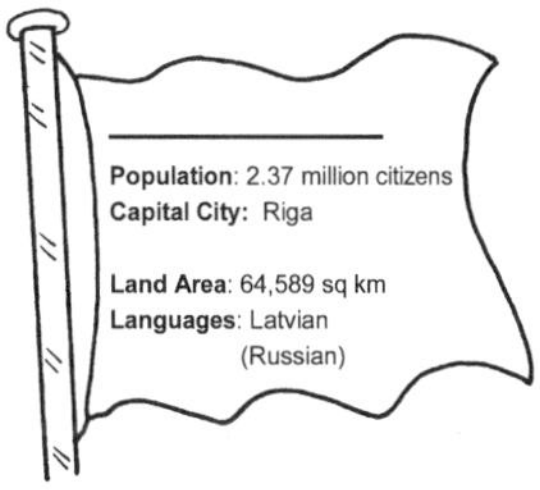

______
Population: 2.37 million citizens
Capital City: Riga
Land Area: 64,589 sq km
Languages: Latvian (Russian)

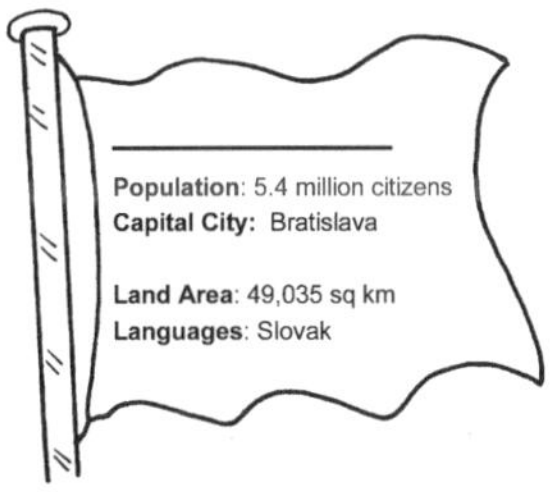

______
Population: 5.4 million citizens
Capital City: Bratislava
Land Area: 49,035 sq km
Languages: Slovak

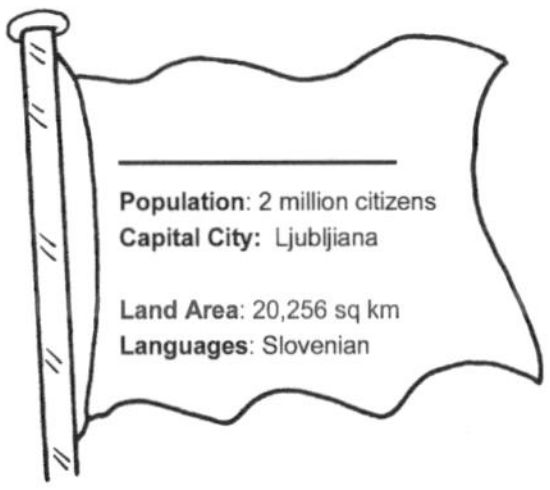

______
Population: 2 million citizens
Capital City: Ljubljiana
Land Area: 20,256 sq km
Languages: Slovenian

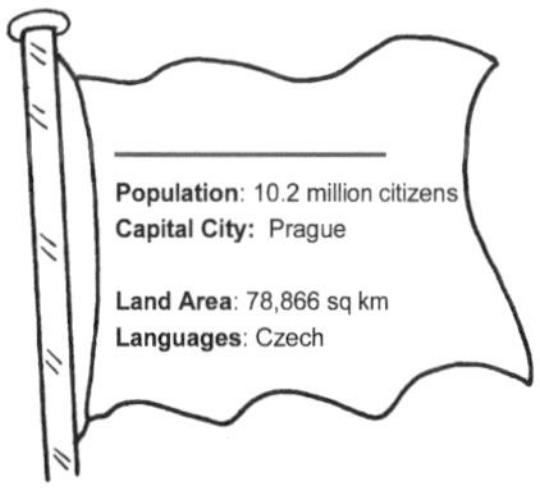

______
Population: 10.2 million citizens
Capital City: Prague
Land Area: 78,866 sq km
Languages: Czech

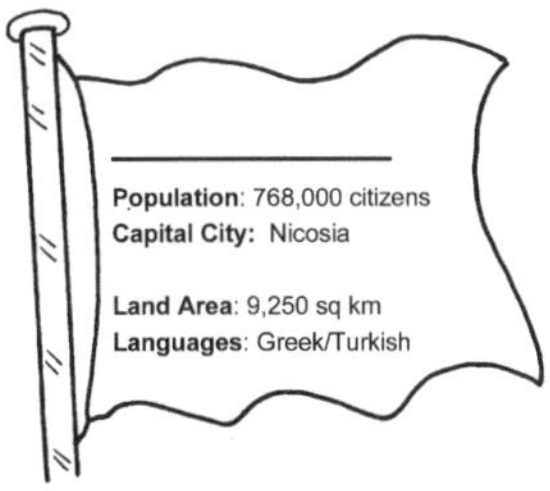

______
Population: 768,000 citizens
Capital City: Nicosia
Land Area: 9,250 sq km
Languages: Greek/Turkish

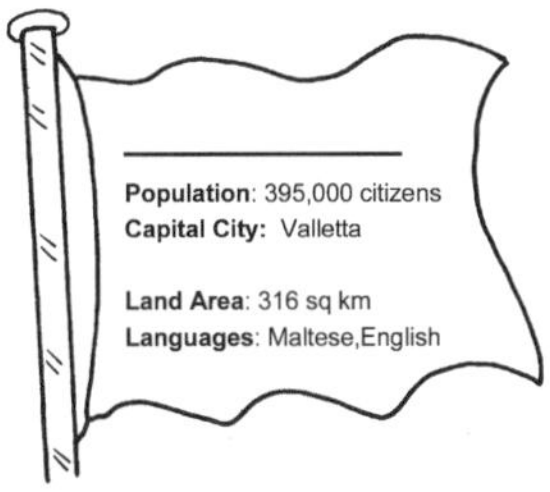

______
Population: 395,000 citizens
Capital City: Valletta
Land Area: 316 sq km
Languages: Maltese,English

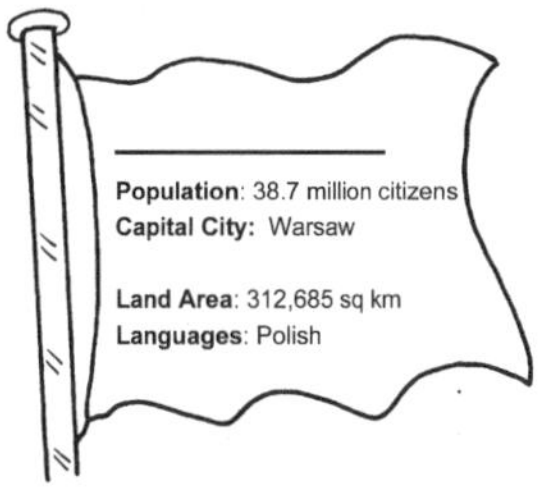

______
Population: 38.7 million citizens
Capital City: Warsaw
Land Area: 312,685 sq km
Languages: Polish

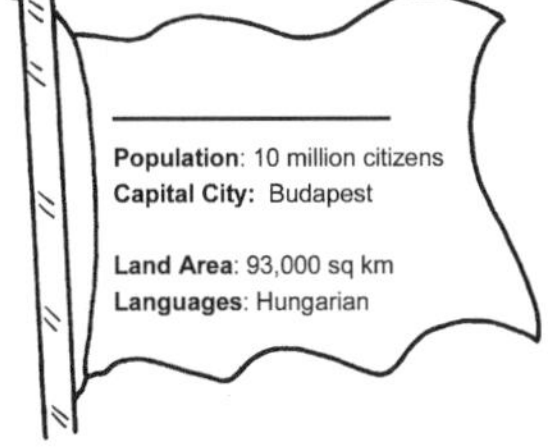

______
Population: 10 million citizens
Capital City: Budapest
Land Area: 93,000 sq km
Languages: Hungarian

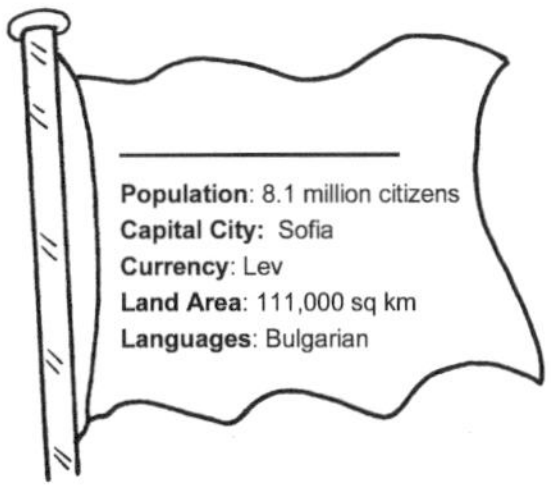

______
Population: 8.1 million citizens
Capital City: Sofia
Currency: Lev
Land Area: 111,000 sq km
Languages: Bulgarian

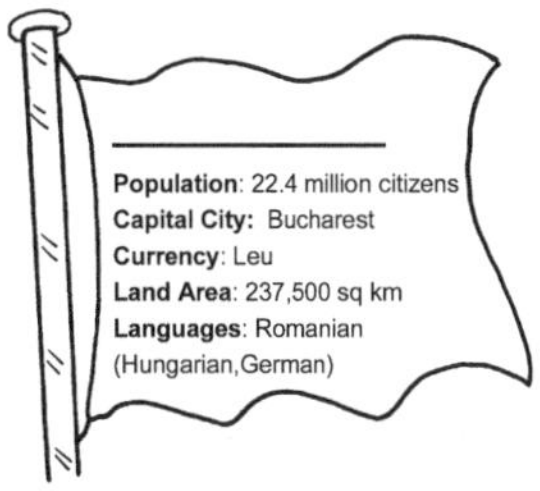

______
Population: 22.4 million citizens
Capital City: Bucharest
Currency: Leu
Land Area: 237,500 sq km
Languages: Romanian (Hungarian,German)

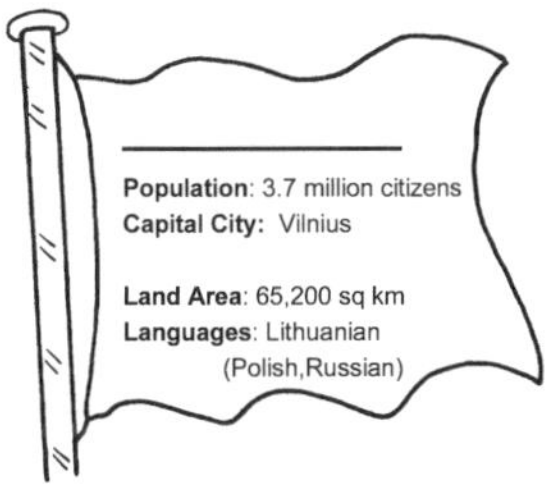

Exercise 2: Euro Quiz

Some of the answers to this quiz can be found in the last exercise.

1. In which country would you dance the flamenco?

2. In which country would you visit the Acropolis?

3. In which country would you visit the Child of Prague?

4. In which country would you eat a baguette or go to see the Mona Lisa?

5. In which country would you be if you found yourself in the city of Bratislava?

6. In which country would you eat sauerkraut and sausage?

7. In which country would you be if you were in the city of Riga?

8. In which country would you be if you took a stroll in the largest park in Europe?

9. In which country would you be if you found yourself in the city of Tallinn?

10. In which country would you be if you crossed from Denmark and got off the train in Malmö?

11. In which country would you be if you found yourself in the city of Ljubljana?

12. In which country would you be if you found yourself in front of the European Court of Justice?

____

13. In which country would you see Big Ben?

____

14. In which country would you be if you found yourself in the city of Warsaw?

____

15. Which country might remind you of Mozart and ski resorts?

____

16. On which island country would you be if you found yourself in the city of Nicosia?

____

17. In which country would you travel along canals in the capital and visit tulip farms?

____

18. On which island country would you be if you found yourself in the city of Valletta?

____

19. In which country would you see the famous statue of the Little Mermaid?

____

20. In which country would you travel by gondola under the Bridge of Sighs?

____

21. In which country could you eat delicious handmade chocolate?

____

22. In which country would you find the manufacturer of Nokia mobile phones?

____

23. In which country would you find a sun-soaked coastline called the Algarve?

____

24. In which country would you be if you found yourself in the city of Budapest?

____

25. In which country would you be if you found yourself in the city of Vilnius?

____

Total score: $\frac{\quad}{25}$

Exercise 3: Who does what in the EU?

Match the names of the European institutions with the correct description of the work it does by drawing a line between them.

- Suggests/proposes new laws and makes sure any agreements are carried out.
- Has the final say on what becomes EU law.
- Has the power to request a member state to change any law that is not in keeping with EU law and can fine any member state that fails to do so.
- Makes sure that the EU budget is properly spent.
- Debates the suggestions and proposals for new laws in Strasbourg.
- Tries to find solutions to issues that are causing difficulty in the EU by holding summit meetings in the country that holds the presidency – this changes every six months.

Exercise 4: United Nations Development Report

This is the UN logo. The world is cradled by two olive branches, suggesting peace.

You may have wondered where people come up with facts and figures about how the world is developing and which parts of the world are suffering from a lack of development. A reliable source of information is the *United Nations Human Development Index*, which is published every year and includes information such as life expectancy at birth, numbers of boys and girls in education, population growth, average income per person, how many doctors per thousand people, figures on internet use per country, etc.

Look at the figures on this gender-related development index and answer the question below.

Country	Life expectancy at birth		Adult literacy rate		Estimated earned income (US$)	
	Male	Female	Male	Female	Male	Female
Norway	75.4	81.3	99%	99%	34,960	22,037
Saudi Arabia	70.3	72.7	83.5%	65.9%	17,857	2,715
Japan	77.3	84.1	99%	99%	35,018	15,187
Yemen	59	61.2	66.6%	23.9%	1,272	345
Ireland	73.8	79.1	99%	99%	37,641	14,347
Burkina Faso	45	47	33%	13.3%	1,177	766

Source: *UN Development Report 2001*

1. In which country would you live the longest?

2. Which country has the lowest literacy rate for women?

3. Which country has the shortest life expectancy for women?

4. Does any of the information on this chart surprise you? Give your reasons why.

OVER SEVENTY PER CENT OF THE 1.5 BILLION PEOPLE IN POVERTY WORLDWIDE ARE WOMEN.

WOMEN MAKE UP OVER FIFTY PER CENT OF THE WORLD'S POPULATION, EARN TEN PER CENT OF THE WORLD'S WAGES AND OWN ONE PER CENT OF THE WORLD'S PROPERTY.

5. If women make up 50 per cent of the world's population, can you think of any reasons why they own only 1 per cent of the world's property?

Exercise 5: United Nations Logos

The United Nations has a number of special agencies that try to help find solutions to global problems.

1. Match the logo to the correct UN organisation/agency. The first one has been done for you.

World Health Organisation

United Nations Development Programme

Food and Agriculture Organisation of the United Nations

United Nations International Research and Training Institute for the Advancement of Women

United Nations International Children's Emergency Fund

Office of the United Nations High Commission for Refugees

2. Redesign the logo of UNEP (United Nations Environment Programme) below.

Existing logo

Your logo

Exercise 6: Goals

In 2000, 189 members of the United Nations signed the Millennium Development Goals. These goals are about ending world poverty, and targets have been set for 2015.

1. Can you match the Millennium Development Goals with the facts in the opposite column?

Goal	
Goal 1	Reduce poverty
Goal 2	Educate every child
Goal 3	Provide equal chances for girls and women
Goal 4	Reduce the numbers of babies and children who die
Goal 5	Ensure a safe and healthy motherhood
Goal 6	Fight diseases like HIV/AIDS and malaria
Goal 7	Clean up the environment
Goal 8	Share responsibility for making the world a better place

Fact
Fact A: In 2000, every 14 seconds another child became an orphan due to an AIDS-related death.
Fact B: If rich countries made trade fairer, poor countries could earn up to $700 billion a year.
Fact C: 64 per cent of the world's adults who cannot read and write are women.
Fact D: 1.2 billion people live on less than €1 a day.
Fact E: 115 million children of primary school age are not in school.
Fact F: Every year more than 5 million women die as a result of pregnancy and childbirth.
Fact G: Every year more than 10 million babies and children die, many from preventable diseases.
Fact H: 1 in 5 children in the developing world do not have clean water.

Adapted from 'Chinya', a CSPE resource produced by Trócaire

Exercise 7: United Nations Quiz

1. What is the General Assembly? ______________________

____

____

____

2. Who is the UN General Secretary?

____

____

3. What is the main aim of the Security Council?

____

____

4. How many members does the UN Security Council have?

____

5. Name one of the permanent members of the Security Council.

____

6. Where are the UN headquarters?

____

7. What is the full name of the UN organisation UNHCR?

____

8. Who wears blue helmets with a UN crest on them?

____

9. What is 10 December dedicated to by the United Nations?

____

10. Can you name a famous Irish person who has held a major job in the United Nations?

____

11. How many member states are there in the United Nations?

____

12. Name a famous UN Goodwill Ambassador. ______________________

____

See *Impact!*, pp 162–168 to help you with your quiz.

Total score: $\frac{\quad}{12}$

Exercise 8: Refugee? Asylum Seeker? Internally Displaced Person?

There are many different reasons why people move around the world. Sometimes they are fleeing from war and persecution, sometimes they are looking for a better way of life.

Read the following profiles of Himpka, Sam, Mohammed, Matthew and Michelle.

Profiles	**Descriptions**
1. As a result of war in Kosovo, Himpka was invited by the Irish government to come and live in Ireland.	C. An internally displaced person
2. When the factory Sam worked in closed down in Limerick he saw lots of advertisements in the paper for jobs in New York. He decided to move there in search of better job opportunities.	D. An asylum seeker
3. When fighting broke out in Kabul, Mohammed was forced to leave his home in the capital of Afghanistan and hide in the mountains of the north.	B. A programme refugee
	A. An economic migrant
4. When the rebels got near their village, Matthew and his mother fled Sierra Leone. They stowed away on a ship going to France. Their uncle who was already in France took them in.	E. A refugee
5. Michelle left Algeria because of religious persecution. When she reached Ireland she went straight to the Department of Justice and stated that she wished to apply to live in Ireland.	

1. Match the profiles to the descriptions given.

Himpka	B
Sam	
Mohammed	
Matthew	
Michelle	

2. Why did Michelle, Sam and Mohammed leave their homes?

   a) Michelle ______________________________

   b) Sam ______________________________

   c) Mohammed ______________________________

3. Name **two** other reasons why people might be forced to leave their own homes.

   a) ______________________________

   b) ______________________________

Exercise 9: How does it Feel?

The United Nations has a number of special agencies that try to solve world problems. One of these agencies is the United Nations High Commission for Refugees. Part of the work that it does is to highlight the difficulties faced by refugees around the world.

Read the message on this poster and answer the following questions.

HOW DOES IT FEEL?

Imagine this.

You've lived all your life at peace. Home, family, friends, all normal. Then, without warning, your whole world changes.

Overnight, lifelong neighbors become enemies. Tanks prowl the streets and buses burn. Mortar shells shatter the mosques. Rockets silence the church bells.

Suddenly everything you've known and owned and loved is gone and, if you're lucky enough to survive, you find yourself alone and bewildered in a foreign land. You are a refugee.

How does it feel?

The fact is, refugees are just like you and me, except that they have been forced to leave their country because of persecution or war. Everything they once had has been lost. And that's exactly why they need our help.

We're not asking for money (though every contribution helps), but only this:

When you meet a refugee, imagine for a moment what it must be like, and then smile. Instead of turning your back.

It may not seem like much. But to a refugee it can mean everything.

UNHCR is a strictly humanitarian organization funded by voluntary contributions. Today, we are helping more than 22 million refugees around the world.

4

1. According to this poster, how do people become refugees?

2. Why does this poster say that refugees need help?

3. What does this poster say you should do when you meet a refugee?

4. Who produced this poster?

5. Do you think that this poster works well to raise awareness about refugees? Explain your answer.

6. Can you name any other organisations that help refugees?

Exercise 10: Does your Wife Work?

Read this story and answer the questions that follow.

'Have you many children?' the doctor asked.

'God has not been good to me. Of sixteen born, only nine live,' he answered.

'Does your wife work?'

'No, she stays at home.'

'I see. How does she spend her day?'

'Well, she gets up in the morning, fetches water and wood, makes the fire and cooks breakfast. Then she goes down to the river and washes clothes. After that she goes to town to get corn ground and buys what we need in the market. Then she cooks the midday meal.'

'You come home at midday?'

'No, no. She brings the meal to me in the fields – about three kilometres from home.'

'And after that?'

'Well, she takes care of the hens and pigs. And of course she looks after the children all day. Then she prepares supper so that it is ready when I come home.'

'Does she go to bed after supper?'

'No, I do. She has things to do around the house until nine o'clock.'

'But you say your wife doesn't work?'

'No, I told you. She stays at home.'

(Source: *International Labour Organisation*)

1. Name six jobs this woman does.

   a) ______________________ d) ______________________

   b) ______________________ e) ______________________

   c) ______________________ f) ______________________

2. Why do you think her husband says she doesn't work?

   ____

   ____

   ____

3. Suggest a way in which the world could change so that women could achieve equality.

   ____

   ____

   ____

Exercise 11: The Red Cross Family

Read the information below about the Red Cross and answer the questions that follow.

The Red Cross was set up by a young Swiss citizen, Henri Dunant, after he witnessed a battle between Austrian and French troops in 1859 that left 36,000 men dead or wounded on the battlefield. He set up a field hospital in a church, and he got helpers to dress wounds, carry water and write farewell letters to the families of dying men. He noticed that all the helpers forgot about the nationality of the men they helped. They were all brothers now. The famous symbol of the Red Cross is the Swiss national flag inverted.

(Adapted from *Exploring Humanitarian Law*, International Committee of the Red Cross)

1. Explain how the Red Cross was started.

____

____

____

The Red Cross Family

National societies like the Irish Red Cross run programmes in health such as first aid, community care, youth work and emergency programmes to help the local population.

The International Federation of Red Cross and Red Crescent societies organises international relief operations in natural disasters.

The International Committee of the Red Cross provides protection and help to victims of armed conflict, without taking sides.

2. Describe some of the work done by the Red Cross Family.

____

____

____

The Red Cross Tracing Service

The Red Cross also has a tracing service to reunite families. In the chaos of armed conflict, families are forced to sell their homes and family members are often separated. More than half of the estimated fifty million refugees and internally displaced people in the world are children and teenagers. More than two million are children who have been separated from their families. As children without parents or carers, they are often subject to abuse and recruitment as child soldiers.

3. What sometimes happens to children in war situations when they have no parents or carers?

____

____

____

The Red Cross Message Service

In wartime, postal services collapse and the only way that families can keep in touch with each other is through the Red Cross Message Service. Using this system, relations write messages, which are then sent by the Red Cross to the families either within the country or in other countries through the network of Red Cross national societies.

Using the Red Cross message form below, write a message to a family member living in another country to tell them that you are OK after the invasion of your country. Remember that Red Cross workers have to check this message. Only personal news is allowed. News about the war/conflict or comments on political matters is not allowed, as the warring parties might object to the message being sent. The Red Cross is a neutral society and does not take sides in conflicts.

Exploration 5D: Focus on restoring family links

Red Cross message form

1. COMITE INTERNATIONAL GENEVE

RED CROSS MESSAGE
MESSAGE CROIX-ROUGE

2. SENDER / EXPEDITEUR

Full name (as expressed locally) / Nom complet (selon l'usage local)

....

Date of birth
Date de naissance .... Sex/Sexe M / F

Father's name
Nom du père ....

Mother's name
Nom de la mère ....

Full address
Adresse complète ....

Province and country
Province et pays ....

3. ADDRESSEE / DESTINATAIRE

Full name (as expressed locally) / Nom complet (selon l'usage local)

....

Date of birth
Date de naissance .... Sex/Sexe M / F

Father's name
Nom du père ....

Mother's name
Nom de la mère ....

Full address
Adresse complète ....

Province and country
Province et pays ....

4. INTERNATIONAL COMMITEE OF THE RED CROSS
COMITE INTERNATIONAL DE LA CROIX-ROUGE
19, av. de la Paix - CH - 1202 GENEVA

5. MESSAGE

(Family and/or private news)
(Nouvelle de caractère personnel et/ou familial)

6. Date .... Signature ....

The addressee is my
Le destinataire est mon/ma ....

Exercise 12: Know Racism

This is the symbol of the Anti-Racist campaign run by the government. The emblem symbolises Five Continents – One World. It was designed by John Rocha.

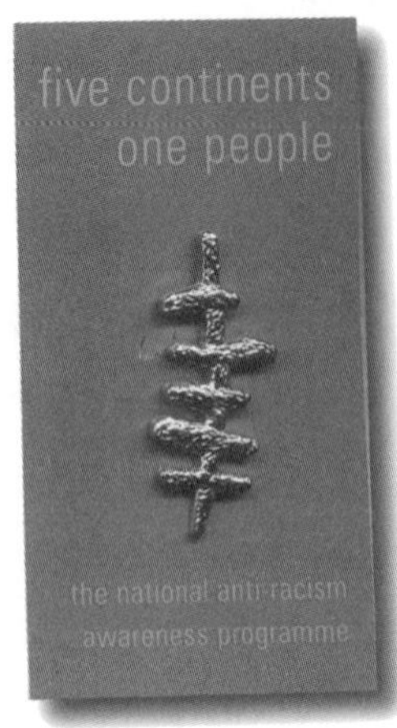

1. Design your own Anti-Racist badge in the space below.

2. Do you think that the slogan for the Anti-Racist campaign is clever? Explain your answer.

____

____

____

____

3. What message does this poster – 'Anti-Racism in the Workplace' – get across?

____

____

____

____

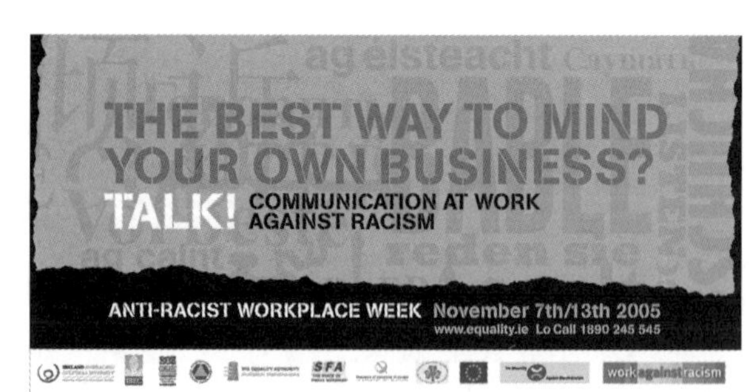

Exercise 13: Anti-Racism Charter

1. Make up an anti-racism charter for your school. You could present this to the school council, or ask your principal to make it an official school policy.

Anti-Racist Charter

In our school we . . .

In our school we . . .

In our school we . . .

In our school we . . .

In our school we . . .

Exercise 14: Different Cultures in our Lives

There are 160 different nationalities now living in Ireland. Each nationality has its own culture and traditions.

1. Think about all the different ways in which different cultures have added to our lives in Ireland, and say where these influences have come from. Look at the pictures to help you with your answers.

Influence	**Culture/Country**
Food	
______________________	______________________
______________________	______________________
Music	
______________________	______________________
______________________	______________________
Clothes	
______________________	______________________
______________________	______________________
Media/TV	
______________________	______________________
______________________	______________________
Leisure	
______________________	______________________
______________________	______________________
Sports	
______________________	______________________
______________________	______________________

MADras Curry

Reggae

Neighbours

2. Can you add any other countries and describe how they have influenced our lives?

____

____

____

(Adapted from *A Young Person's Guide to Cultural Diversity in Northern Ireland*, 1999)

Exercise 15: Fair Play to You!

Sometimes people say that they would like to buy Fair Trade goods but that they are not easy to find in many shops. Read the article on what you can find in the shops run by Amnesty International and answer the questions that follow:

Fair play to you

You too can show support for human rights when you play with a Fair Trade football.

Amnesty's shops enable shoppers to make a difference to the lives of people around the world, while also indulging themselves, just a little bit.

Amnesty has been purchasing Fair Trade footballs since 2000 from a company called Sialkot, who along with the International Labour Organisation and UNICEF is working to eliminate child labour from the soccer ball industry.

Children are forced into labour to help their families survive. While helping their families, many of the children miss out on an education, creating a vicious cycle of poverty and uneducated labour. There are also long-term physical effects from their work including loss of eyesight, chronic back and neck pains, cuts on their fingers and even deformation of their fingers.

You can show support for these children who are being denied their right to be just that, children, by buying Fair Trade soccer balls at www.amnesty.ie or in our shops. Our stores in Dublin and Galway will shortly stock Fair Trade sneakers as well.

And for those of you who prefer to watch sports rather than don the gear, you can spoil yourself with our NEW Fair Trade praline and hazelnut chocolate. Reward yourself for helping others!

www.amnesty.ie 17

1. What has Amnesty been purchasing since 2000?

____

2. What are the effects on children who have been forced into labour?

____

____

____

3. What will Amnesty stores in Dublin and Galway be stocking shortly?

____

____

____

Exercise 16: The Way We Live – Global Problems

Read the speech bubbles to find out what these people think are world problems.

1. Name the issues these people have spoken about.

 a) ______________________________

 b) ______________________________

 c) ______________________________

 d) ______________________________

 e) ______________________________

2. Can you name another global problem?

____

____

____

____

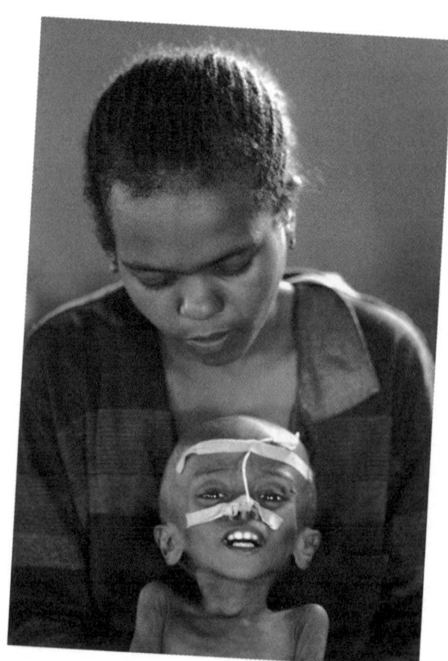

'The future is not a gift: it is an achievement. Every generation helps make its own future. This is the essential challenge of the present.'

Robert F. Kennedy, Address to the Seattle World Fair, 1962

3. Choose any issue and suggest **two** actions you could take to highlight the issue.

Issue: ______________________________

____

____

____

____

____

Action 1: ______________________________

____

____

____

____

____

Action 2: ______________________________

____

____

____

____

____

Exercise 17: The Work of ActionAid Ireland

All the Irish NGOs are working hard to see that the Millennium Development Goals become a reality. ActionAid International Ireland is very concerned about the education goals. Read the following case study and answer the questions that follow.

Molly Nantongo is from Uganda. She is 23 years old. Molly had to leave school ten years ago to care for her younger brothers and sisters after both her parents died from AIDS. Molly had dreamed of becoming a nurse, but now she is one of an estimated 137 million young people starting adult life without even the basic tools of literacy.

ActionAid International Ireland has been involved in securing children's and adults' right to education since 1983. The organisation at present works in:

- Uganda – with out of school disadvantaged children
- Malawi – with teenage girls, their parents and teachers to encourage the girls to stay in secondary school
- Tanzania – to improve working standards and conditions for primary students and teachers
- Vietnam – to provide ethnic minority children with trained teachers and facilities.

The right to education was agreed by world governments in 2000 at the Millennium Summit. Two of the eight Millennium Development Goals (MDGs) agreed at the Summit for ending world poverty are education-related.

Worldwide, groups have come together as the Global Campaign for Education to ensure that governments keep their commitment to ensuring that all the world's children have access to education by 2015.

Every school in Ireland is invited to take part in the Global Week of Action for Education in April of each year. See www.campaignforeducation.ie and www.campaignforeducation.org for details on how to get your class active for an Education For All!

1. Why did Molly have to leave school? ______

2. What were Molly's dreams? ______

3. What kind of work has ActionAid International Ireland been doing?

4. How many of the Millennium Development goals have to do with education?

5. How can schools get involved in the Global Campaign for Education?

6. Why do you think that education for all is an important goal?
Give **two** reasons for your answer.

Exercise 18: Extract from a Speech by Robert Kennedy

The following is an extract from a speech by Robert F. Kennedy given in the University of Cape Town, South Africa in 1962, known as the **Day of Affirmation Address**.

Robert Kennedy was the younger brother of John F. Kennedy, President of the United States. He was the youngest Attorney General in the history of the USA. He was assassinated, like his brother, while campaigning to become President of the United States.

'Many of the world's greatest movements, of thought and action, have flowed from the work of a single man. A young monk began the Protestant Reformation, and a young woman reclaimed the territory of France. It was a young Italian explorer who discovered the New World, and 32-year-old Thomas Jefferson who proclaimed that all men are created equal. "Give me a place to stand," said Archimedes*, "and I will move the world." These men moved the world, and so can we all. Few will have the greatness to bend history; but each of us can work to change a small portion of events, and in the total of all these acts will be written the history of this generation ...

Thousands of unknown men and women in Europe resisted the occupation of the Nazis and many died, but all added to the ultimate strength and freedom of their countries ... Each time a man stands up for an ideal, or acts to improve the lot of others, or strikes out against injustice, he sends forth a tiny ripple of hope ... those ripples build a current which can sweep down the mightiest walls of oppression and resistance.'

*Archimedes was a Greek mathematician.

1. According to this speech by Robert F. Kennedy, how have many of the world's greatest movements started?

____

____

2. Name **three** people that Robert Kennedy uses as examples of people who have changed the world in some way.

   a) ______________________________________

   b) ______________________________________

   c) ______________________________________

3. What does Kennedy think that each person can do to help write the history of their generation?

____

____

____

4. According to Kennedy, how is it possible to 'send forth a tiny ripple of hope'?

____

____

____

5. Can you think of any other people who have helped to change the world for the better in some way?

____

____

____

6. 'Ask not what your country can do for you, but what you can do for your country' (J. F. Kennedy). Do you think that this was a good message to give to citizens? Give reasons for your answer.

____

____

____

Exercise 19: Revision

Ordering History

This is a short history of the European Union. The events are not shown in the order in which they happened.

Put them in the correct order by filling in the numbers 1–8 in the right-hand column.

A. Amsterdam Treaty (1999)	
B. Ireland joins the EEC (1973)	
C. Maastricht Treaty (1993)	
D. Treaty of Paris (1951)	1
E. Nice Treaty (2002)	
F. The EEC becomes the European Community (1987)	
G. The euro is introduced (2002)	
H. Treaty of Rome (1957)	

European Union Word Search

S	P	A	E	C	G	N	G	L	C	A	F	Q	B	L
A	L	Y	L	D	S	H	K	P	O	M	W	C	D	I
T	N	E	D	I	S	E	R	P	M	G	V	Z	S	C
R	H	Z	S	X	Z	J	U	O	M	B	U	T	Q	N
P	V	F	T	S	Q	K	Y	I	I	S	R	W	Q	U
H	A	F	P	E	U	P	S	Y	S	A	S	R	O	O
M	J	R	A	W	W	R	J	U	S	Q	P	H	Z	C
M	D	S	L	P	V	K	B	B	I	C	H	O	H	S
Y	K	Q	C	I	T	G	O	J	O	O	R	Z	E	W
A	Q	H	P	D	A	U	O	C	N	B	P	T	D	Q
T	R	J	Q	W	R	M	D	W	U	Q	O	F	S	L
L	Z	L	N	G	S	Y	E	I	T	V	P	W	X	C
L	W	S	O	Q	R	H	A	N	X	G	N	L	O	S
B	K	G	F	D	S	U	K	P	T	M	G	Z	D	E
M	O	V	F	R	R	V	M	F	D	N	O	M	E	P

Find these words in the grid above.

BRUSSELS
COMMISSION
COUNCIL
MEP
PARLIAMENT
PRESIDENT
STRASBOURG
VOTE

European Union Word Grid

Use the clues below to fill in the word grid.

Across

1. You can send one of these to the European Parliament.
2. Ireland got money from this fund to build roads.
4. Pat Cox was elected to do this job for two years.
5. You elect MEPs by doing this.

Down

1. This European institution debates new laws.
3. This European institution has the final say on what becomes EU law.

Global Issues Word Grid

Use the clues below to fill in the word grid.

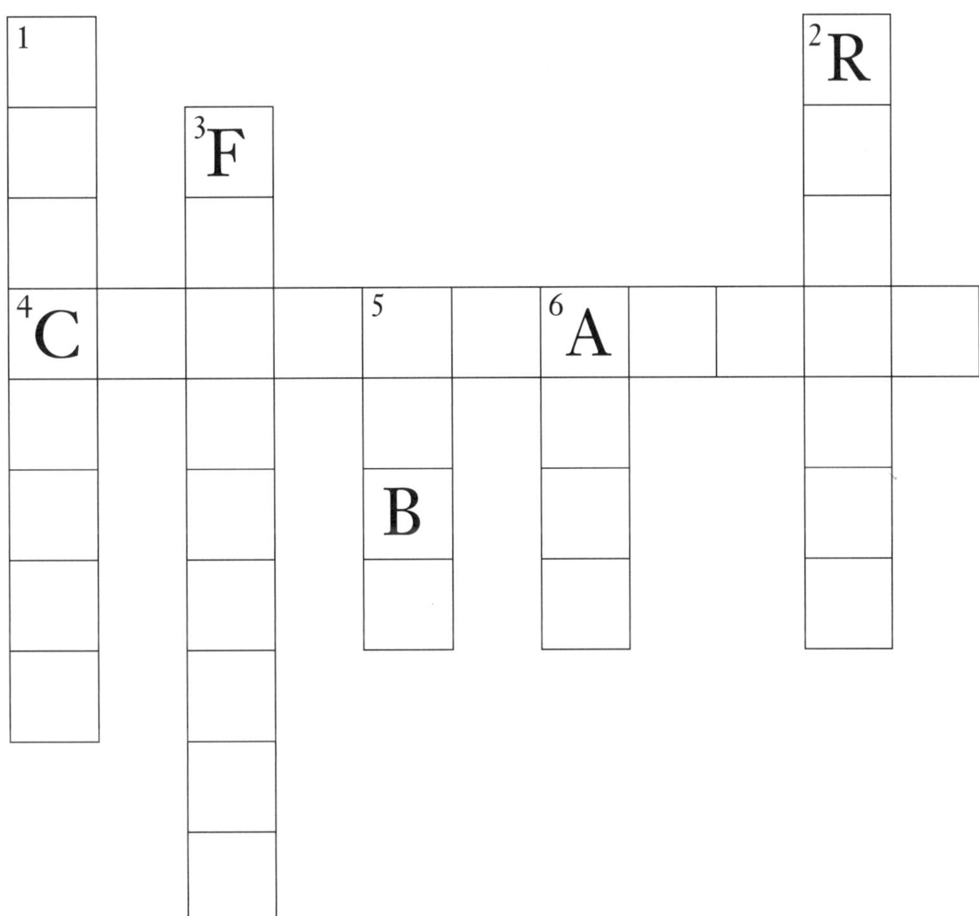

Across

4. Some carpet factories use them as workers.

Down

1. An Irish aid agency.
2. A person who is forced to leave their country.
3. This means workers receiving fair wages for products.
5. Many countries in the developing world are repaying this.
6. $2 billion is spent buying these every day.

CSPE Concepts Word Search

1. Find the seven CSPE concepts in the word search below.

DEVELOPMENT	INTERDEPENDENCE	RIGHTS
LAW	STEWARDSHIP	RESPONSIBILITIES
DEMOCRACY	DIGNITY	

B	I	S	R	H	X	A	A	K	U	B	Z	P	K	T	R
T	Z	F	I	X	Z	U	Y	O	K	G	J	Z	O	U	E
A	I	P	G	F	X	S	L	Y	C	C	T	X	F	H	S
R	P	N	H	Y	D	J	C	H	T	A	A	R	Z	T	P
U	O	S	T	E	W	A	R	D	S	H	I	P	X	I	O
J	E	C	S	E	R	V	B	C	Z	T	U	O	R	O	N
V	I	C	K	C	R	F	K	E	F	Y	I	P	T	Y	S
I	N	L	O	V	F	D	R	W	G	D	R	X	D	R	I
R	A	M	R	M	C	S	E	B	N	U	G	U	Y	J	B
H	E	D	E	V	E	L	O	P	M	E	N	T	W	Z	I
D	C	L	T	K	S	G	A	V	E	Z	I	V	W	K	L
J	O	Z	D	D	R	L	J	W	U	N	Z	A	P	I	I
V	M	J	U	G	Y	D	L	X	G	L	C	N	U	N	T
U	Z	C	Q	P	M	D	H	I	R	M	A	E	J	M	I
F	O	V	D	G	O	M	D	I	H	R	U	V	A	F	E
G	H	I	K	O	U	S	I	P	H	R	W	S	T	I	S

Put each of the concepts shown in the box below into a sentence to show what it means.

1. ____

____

2. ____

____

3. ____

____

4. ____

____

5. ____

____

6. ____

____

7. ____

____

LAW	DEMOCRACY
RIGHTS AND RESPONSIBILITIES	HUMAN DIGNITY
INTERDEPENDENCE	DEVELOPMENT
STEWARDSHIP	

CSPE

Sample Exam Papers

Coimisiún na Scrúduithe Stáit
State Examinations Commission

JUNIOR CERTIFICATE EXAMINATION, 2004

CIVIC, SOCIAL AND POLITICAL EDUCATION

FRIDAY, 11 JUNE – AFTERNOON 2.00–3.30

INSTRUCTIONS

Answer **all questions** in Section 1	(18 marks)
Answer **any three questions** in Section 2	(42 marks)
Answer **any one question** in Section 3	(20 marks)
Total	(80 marks)

SECTION 1

Answer ALL the questions in this section.

1. The following photographs show four political leaders who each work in, or have worked in, one of the four famous buildings listed below. Put the correct name of the building they each work in, or have worked in, opposite their photograph.

You may use the name of each building only ONCE.

Buildings:	Áras an Uachtaráin	The White House
	No. 10 Downing St.	Leinster House

(a) ______________________________

(b) ______________________________

(c) ______________________________

(d) ______________________________

(4 marks)

2. **Name of Organisation:**

Trócaire

Amnesty International

The Simon Community

Irish Society for the Prevention of Cruelty to Children (ISPCC).

Each of the descriptions given below describes the work of **ONE** of the organisations listed above. Beside each description write the name of the organisation you think it describes.

You may write ONE name only beside each description.

Description of organisation's work	**Name of organisation**
Campaigns against cruelty to children	
Works mainly with people in the developing world	
Looks after the needs of the homeless in Ireland	
Draws attention to abuses of human rights in a different countries	

(4 marks)

3. Write a sentence to explain **EACH** of the following:

Dáil Éireann is ______________________________

____

____

Seanad Éireann is ______________________________

____

____

Bunreacht na hÉireann is ______________________________

____

____

Áras an Uachtaráin is ______________________________

____

____

An Taoiseach is ____

____

____

(5 marks)

4. Name **FIVE** countries that became full members of the European Union in May 2004:

(a) ____

(b) ____

(c) ____

(d) ____

(e) ____

(5 marks)

SECTION 2

Answer any THREE of the questions numbered 1, 2, 3, 4 below.

Each question carries 14 marks

1. **Electronic Voting**

Study the picture that is printed on page 122.

On the top of the page you will read "Electronic Voting – picture for Section 2, Question 1."

When you have studied this picture, answer the questions below.

(a) What kind of vote is taking place in this picture? Put a tick (✓) in the box next to the answer that you think is correct. Tick (✓) **ONE** box only.

A General Election vote ☐

A Referendum vote ☐

(1 mark)

(b) Give **ONE** reason for your answer.

____

____

____

(1 mark)

(c) What is the difference between "electronic voting" and the voting system used up to now?

____

____

____

(2 marks)

(d) Give **ONE** advantage and **ONE** disadvantage of electronic voting.

One advantage is ________________________________

____

One disadvantage is ______________________________

____

(4 marks)

(e) When electronic voting was first introduced in 2002 it was put into operation in only three of the forty-one electoral constituencies. Give **ONE** reason why you think it was tried only in three constituencies.

One reason is __________________________________

____

(2 marks)

(f) Apart from a general election and a referendum, name **TWO** other types of elections that the Government can call.

Type of election 1 ______________________________

Type of election 2 ______________________________

(4 marks)

2. **Headlines**

Study the selection of newspaper headlines that is printed on page 122. On the page you will read "Headlines for Section 2, Question 2."

When you have studied these headlines, answer the questions below.

(a) Who is seeking talks with Ahern? ____________________

What type of centre is to close? ____________________

What organisation has missed its target for recycling? ____________________

(3 marks)

(b) Name **TWO** issues mentioned in these headlines.

First issue ____________________

Second issue ____________________

(2 marks)

(c) If you were to organise a campaign on **ONE** of these issues with your CSPE class, name and briefly explain **TWO** actions that you would take to get the campaign going.

Name of first action ____________________

Explanation ____________________

____

____

Name of second action ____________________

____

____

Explanation ____________________

(4 marks)

(d) In 2003 the European Union organised a campaign called the *European Year of People with Disabilities*. What do you think the purpose of this campaign was?

The purpose of the *European Year of People with Disabilities* campaign was

____

____

____

(2 marks)

(e) State whether you think this campaign was successful or not.

Tick (✓) **ONE** box only.

It was successful ☐

If was not successful ☐

Give **ONE** reason for your answer.

(3 marks)

3. **The Cabinet**

Study the photograph of The Cabinet AND the information about The Cabinet that are printed on page 123. On the top of the page you will read "The Cabinet – picture and information for Section 2, Question 3."

When you have studied this picture and the information answer the questions below.

(a) How many Ministers are in the Cabinet? ______________________

(1 mark)

(b) One of those in the Cabinet is the Minister for Finance. Name the titles of **TWO** other Ministers:

The Minister for ______________________

The Minister for ______________________

(2 marks)

(c) How many of the Ministers in the Cabinet are women? ______________________

(1 mark)

(d) Give **TWO** reasons why there are fewer women than men in politics in Ireland.

First reason ______________________________

Second reason ______________________________

(4 marks)

(e) Describe **TWO** actions that the Government could take to encourage more women to stand for election.

First action ______________________________

Second action ______________________________

(6 marks)

4. Disability – Key Facts

The following set of Key Facts about people with disabilities comes from the National Rehabilitation Board. Study these facts carefully and answer the questions that follow.

Key Facts

- **A survey carried out by the National Rehabilitation Board showed that 70 per cent of those surveyed knew of equipment that would make life easier for them, but almost all could not afford to buy the equipment.**
- **People who get a disability while at work receive higher allowances than people who have been disabled from birth.**
- **Buildings and services often prevent people with disabilities from taking part in everyday life.**

(a) According to the survey, what percentage of people with disabilities could not afford to buy equipment that would make life easier for them? ______________

(2 marks)

(b) What difference is mentioned between people who get a disability at work and those who are disabled from birth?

____

(2 marks)

(c) Give **ONE** example of how either a building **OR** a service can prevent people with disabilities from taking part in everyday life.

____

____

____

(2 marks)

(d) Describe **TWO** actions that a **SCHOOL** could take to improve conditions for students with disabilities.

First action ____

____

____

Second action ____

____

____

(4 marks)

(e) Describe **TWO** actions **YOU** could take to improve the attitudes of your fellow students towards people with disabilities.

First action ____

____

____

Second action ____

____

____

(4 marks)

SECTION 3

Answer ONE of the questions numbered 1, 2, 3, 4 below.

Each question carries 20 marks.

If you need extra paper to answer this question, please ask the Examination Superintendent for it.

1. **Deaths on our roads**

In recent years the Department of the Environment has run advertisement campaigns on television designed to reduce the number of deaths on our roads.

Your CSPE class intends to carry out a survey in your local community to find out peoples' opinions of these advertisement campaigns.

(a) Describe **TWO** classroom activities that you would organise that would help your CSPE class to plan and prepare this survey.

____

____

____

____

____

____

(6 marks)

(b) Write **THREE** questions that you would ask in this survey. Give a reason for asking **EACH** question.

____

____

____

____

____

____

(6 marks)

(c) Describe **TWO** follow-up activities that your CSPE class could undertake that would help publicise your findings.

____

____

____

____

(8 marks)

2. Local Elections

You have been selected by your political party to stand as a party candidate in the local elections.

(a) As a candidate for the local election you have to prepare your campaign. Name **THREE** political issues that you would like to highlight in this election. In the case of **ONE** of these explain why you think it is an important political issue.

____

____

____

____

____

____

____

____

____

____

(8 marks)

(b) Draw a sketch of a poster that you would design for your election campaign. You should include an appropriate slogan in your sketch, as well as an outline drawing or graphic.

(6 marks)

(c) Apart from campaign leaflets and election posters, name and describe **TWO** other ways in which your political party could support you in your election campaign.

____

____

____

____

____

(6 marks)

3. War in Iraq

As part of International Human Rights Day (December 10th) your CSPE class has decided to hold a public exhibition and debate on the causes and effects of the War in Iraq.

(a) For the exhibition you have decided to print a number of posters. Draw an outline of **ONE** of these posters. In your outline you should include the name of a world leader **AND** the reason he/she gave for going to war in Iraq.

(6 marks)

(b) Write a letter to the Ambassador of one of the countries that sent troops to fight in the war inviting him/her to be a member of the team of speakers that will publicly debate the causes and effects of the war.

In your letter, explain to the Ambassador

- why you are inviting him/her to be a member of the debate
- why you think it is important for young people to be properly informed about global issues such as this

AND

- tell him/her the name of **ONE** other organisation you have invited to come to the debate and the reasons why you have invited that organisation.

(6 marks)

(c) Write **FOUR** questions that you would ask the speakers about the war and its effects.

(8 marks)

4. Environmental Disaster

Your family, and other families in your local community, have been affected by an environmental disaster (for example, a landslide, a fire, a flood, or pollution). The families have now decided to set up a local action committee to look for aid. You have been chosen as a youth representativc on this committee.

(a) Name **ONE** organisation that the action committee should ask for aid. Give **TWO** reasons why you think this organisation should be asked.

(6 marks)

(b) Write a short article for your school magazine explaining the purpose of the action committee. In your answer you should mention at least **TWO** different points about the purpose of the committee.

(6 marks)

(c) Describe **TWO** ways in which your school could become involved in helping this action committee.

____

____

____

(8 marks)

Please tick the question from Section 3 that you are answering.

Q.1 ☐ **Q.2** ☐ **Q.3** ☐ **Q.4** ☐

Electronic Voting – picture for Section 2, Question 1.

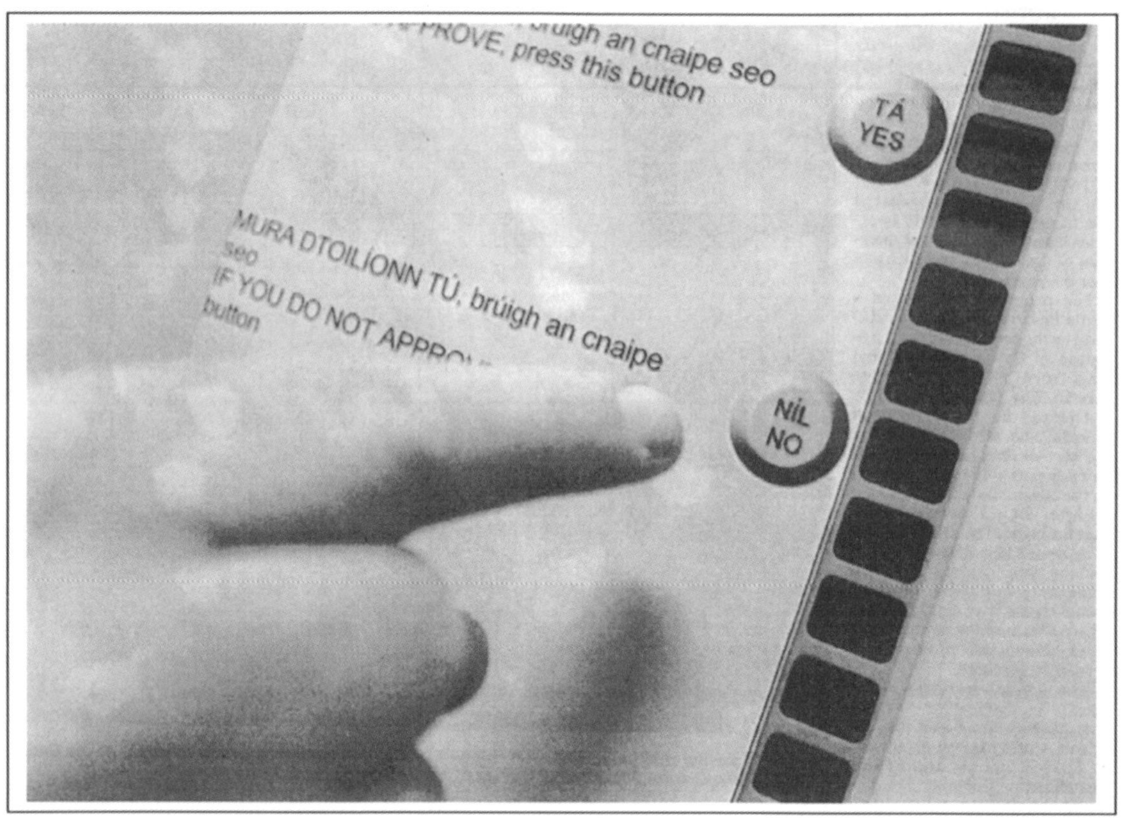

Headlines for Section 2, Question 2.

Garda to get greater powers

€31m in EU emergency aid for fire-hit Portugal

Dublin City Council to miss target for recycling

Young people's homeless centre to close

housing for new asylum-seekers

Disability rights group seeks talks with Ahern

The Cabinet – picture and information for Section 2, Question 3.

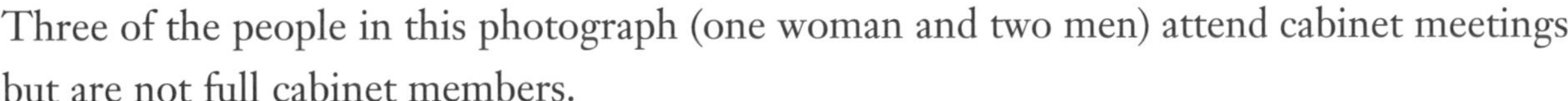

Three of the people in this photograph (one woman and two men) attend cabinet meetings but are not full cabinet members.

The Cabinet:	Total number of Ministers:	15
	Number of Women:	2
	Number of Men:	13

Coimisiún na Scrúduithe Stáit
State Examinations Commission

JUNIOR CERTIFICATE EXAMINATION, 2005

CIVIC, SOCIAL AND POLITICAL EDUCATION

FRIDAY, 10 JUNE – AFTERNOON 2.00–3.30

INSTRUCTIONS

Answer **all questions** in Section 1	(18 marks)
Answer **any three questions** in Section 2	(42 marks)
Answer **any one question** in Section 3	(20 marks)
Total	(80 marks)

IMPORTANT: When you are answering the questions on this paper, you are expected to answer from the human rights approach of the CSPE course.

SECTION 1

Answer ALL of the questions in this section.

1. The following photographs are of four politicians who hold, or who have held, important positions in politics in Ireland. Write down in the space provided the title/position which each politician holds, or has held.

   You may use each title only ONCE.

   Titles/Positions: President of Ireland — Tánaiste — Ceann Comhairle of Dáil Éireann — Taoiseach

(i) ____________________

(ii) ____________________

(iii) ____________________

(iv) ____________________

(4 marks)

2. *CSPE course concepts*

Democracy *Interdependence*

Development *Stewardship*

Each of the meanings given below explains **ONE** of the course concepts listed above. Beside each meaning write the name of the concept you think it explains. **You may write ONE concept only beside each meaning. You may use each concept only ONCE.**

Meaning of Concept	Course Concept
Caring responsibly for our environment and the planet on which we live	
Government by the people, through voting and elections	
Improvements taking place in communities at home and abroad	
The ways in which we are connected with others in the world	

(4 marks)

3. Below are the names of six political parties. The names of six people who lead, or who have led, a political party in Ireland are also listed below. Write the name of **EACH** political party opposite its leader. **You may write only ONE party opposite each leader**.

Political Parties

Fianna Fáil *Sinn Féin* *The Labour Party*

Fine Gael *The Green Party* *The Progressive Democrats*

Party leader	**The party led by this person is**
Gerry Adams	______________________
Bertie Ahern	______________________
Mary Harney	______________________
Enda Kenny	______________________
Pat Rabbitte	______________________
Trevor Sargent	______________________

(6 marks)

4. (a) An Tánaiste is the ...

Put a tick [✓] in the box opposite the **ONE** answer you think is correct.

(i) Deputy Prime Minister ☐

(ii) Irish Constitution ☐

(iii) Home of the President ☐

(iv) Chairperson of the Seanad ☐

(b) The Dáil and Seanad meet in ...

Put a tick [✓] in the box opposite the **ONE** answer you think is correct.

(i) Farmleigh House ☐

(ii) Stormont Castle ☐

(iii) Leinster House ☐

(iv) Áras an Uachtaráin ☐

(c) How many Dáil constituencies are there?

Put a tick [✓] in the box opposite the **ONE** answer you think is correct.

(i) 13 ☐

(ii) 32 ☐

(iii) 40 ☐

(iv) 43 ☐

(d) How many MEPs (Members of the European Parliament) did the Republic of Ireland elect in 2004?

Put a tick [✓] in the box opposite the **ONE** answer you think is correct.

(i) 13 ☐

(ii) 18 ☐

(iii) 25 ☐

(iv) 40 ☐

(4 marks)

SECTION 2

Answer any THREE of the questions numbered 1, 2, 3, 4 below.

Each question carries 14 marks.

1. ***The 60th Anniversary of the death of Anne Frank***

Study the Anne Frank Information Sheet printed on page 137. On the top of the page you will read 'Anne Frank Information Sheet for Section 2, Question 1'. When you have studied this information sheet, answer the questions below.

(a) How many years ago was Anne Frank born?

____

Where did Anne Frank die in March 1945?

____

According to the information sheet, what is Anne Frank famous for?

____

____

(3 marks)

(b) Anne Frank House is now a museum. Name the **THREE** concepts it is trying to promote.

First Concept ____

Second Concept ____

Third Concept ____

(3 marks)

(c) Reading Anne Frank's life story can help us realise the value of tolerance and respect and the importance of human rights. Name **TWO** important documents drawn up by the United Nations to protect human rights.

Document One ____

Document Two ____

(2 marks)

(d) The Information Sheet says that the discrimination and racism that brought an end to Anne's life did not disappear with the end of World War II. Today people are still being persecuted and murdered because they, just like Anne Frank, are 'different'.

Name **TWO** groups of people in Ireland who may have experienced discrimination.

Group One ____

Group Two ____

(2 marks)

(e) Describe **TWO** actions **YOUR SCHOOL** could take to encourage students in Ireland to be more tolerant and respectful of people who are 'different'.

First action ____

Second action ____

(4 marks)

2. ***Student Councils***

Study the Student Council brochure printed on page 138. On the top of the page you will read 'Student Council Brochure for Section 2, Question 2'. When you have studied this brochure, answer the questions below.

(a) What is a Student Council?

____

____

____

____

What Act states that Boards of Management must encourage the setting up of Student Councils in schools?

____

(3 marks)

(b) What does the National Children's Strategy state about children and young people?

____

____

____

____

(2 marks)

(c) Your CSPE class has decided to organise a campaign to set up a Student Council in your school. Name and explain **TWO** actions that your CSPE class could take as part of this campaign.

First action ________________________________

Explanation ________________________________

Second action ________________________________

Explanation ________________________________

(4 marks)

(d) Suggest a slogan that would help students to understand the **importance** of a Student Council for your school.

____

____

(2 marks)

(e) Name **THREE** important issues for students that the Student Council might discuss at its meetings.

First Issue ________________________________

Second Issue ________________________________

Third Issue ________________________________

(3 marks)

3. *Child Labour*

Study the Stop Child Labour poster printed on page 139. On the top of the page you will read 'Child Labour Poster for Section 2, Question 3'. When you have studied this poster, answer the questions below.

(a) Child Labour denies children the right to what?

____

How many young people between the ages of 5 and 17 are defined as child labourers?

____

What is the website address for this campaign to stop child labour?

____

(3 marks)

(b) Name **THREE** different types of work in which child labourers are involved.

First Type ________________________________

Second Type ________________________________

Third Type ________________________________

(3 marks)

(c) The Protection of Young Persons (Employment) Act, 1996 states that the maximum weekly working hours are 0 hours for 14 year olds and 8 hours for 15 years olds during school term-time and 35 hours per week during holidays. Give **ONE** reason why you think this law was brought in.

____

____

____

(2 marks)

(d) The International Labour Organisation estimates that 246 million children between the ages of 5 and 17 years of age are working as child labourers. Most of these children are in Asia (60%) and in Africa (32%).

Suggest **ONE** action **THE IRISH GOVERNMENT** could take to help reduce the number of child labourers.

____

____

(2 marks)

(e) As a citizen of Ireland you also can play a role. Suggest **TWO** actions **YOU** could take to inform people in your community about Child Labour.

First action __________________________________

____

____

____

Second action ________________________________

____

____

____

(4 marks)

4. ***Trading Fairly***

Study the Trading Fairly page printed on page 140. On the top of the page you will read 'Trading Fairly Page for Section 2, Question 4'. When you have studied the page, answer the questions below.

(a) The article is about a campaign to do with trading fairly. Name the group organising the campaign.

Group ______________________________

What does Fairtrade guarantee? ______________________________

____

(2 marks)

(b) Give **ONE** reason why the wages of Tea Pluckers are so low.

Reason ______________________________

____

____

____

(2 marks)

(c) Fairtrade Tea Pluckers get a bonus. Why is this very important to them?

____

____

____

(4 marks)

(d) Name **TWO** Fairtrade Mark foods that are available in Ireland.

First Food ______________________________

Second Food ______________________________

(2 marks)

(e) In March each year Fairtrade Fortnight is held in Ireland to promote Fairtrade. Describe **TWO** actions your CSPE class could take to promote Fairtrade in your school as part of Fairtrade Fortnight.

First action ______________________________

____

____

____

Second action ______________________________

____

____

____

(4 marks)

SECTION 3

Answer ONE of the questions numbered 1, 2, 3, 4 below.
Each question carries 20 marks.
A blank page for the poster questions has been included at the back of this answer book.
If you need extra paper to answer this question, please ask the Examination Superintendent for it.

1. *Celebrate Earth Day*

Senator Nelson, an American politician, thought up the idea of having a special day to do something about what is happening to the environment. The first Earth Day happened in the USA on 22 April 1970 and is now celebrated around the world on that date.

As part of your learning about stewardship of the environment your CSPE class has decided to celebrate Earth Day.

(a) Draw a sketch of a poster that you would use to raise awareness about Earth Day. You should include a suitable slogan in your sketch, with a drawing or picture. (A blank page for the poster has been included at the back of this answerbook). (6 marks)

(b) Write a short article for your school magazine explaining why Earth Day is important. In your article mention at least **TWO** different reasons for getting involved. (6 marks)

(c) Describe **TWO** practical actions your CSPE class could take on Earth Day to encourage people in your community to look after their environment. (8 marks)

2. *Save The Round Tower Campaign*

There is a round tower in your area that has survived the attacks of the Vikings. This tower is under threat if a planning application for a development of shops and businesses gets the go-ahead from the local authority.

You and members of your community agree that this tower is of great benefit to the community.

(a) Write **THREE** arguments that you would put in a campaign leaflet to stop the planned development in your area. (6 marks)

(b) Write a letter to your local authority objecting to the proposed development. In your letter suggest **TWO** other development proposals for this important site. Explain how these developments will be good for the community. (6 marks)

(c) Describe **TWO** actions that your community could undertake as part of its campaign to save the round tower. (8 marks)

3. ***Mock Election***

Imagine that an election is taking place in Ireland at the moment. You and your classmates have suggested that your CSPE class hold a mock election for the whole school.

(a) Suggest **TWO** reasons why this mock election would be a good action project for all students in the school.

(6 marks)

(b) Draw a sketch of a poster that you would use to encourage young people in your school to vote in the mock election. You should include a suitable slogan in your sketch, with a drawing or picture. (A blank page for the poster has been included at the back of this answerbook).

(6 marks)

(c) Describe the work of **THREE** Committees that you would set up in order to organise the mock election.

(8 marks)

4. ***A Visit to a Court House* or *a Prison***

Your CSPE class has just completed work on 'The Law in Our Lives' and you have decided to organise a visit to a Court House **or** a Prison to see the Irish justice system in action.

(a) Describe the work of **THREE** Committees you would set up in order to plan and organise the visit. (State clearly which place you plan to visit.)

(8 marks)

(b) Write **THREE** questions that you would ask your guide on the visit in order to develop your understanding of the law in Ireland.

(6 marks)

(c) Describe **TWO** follow-up activities that your CSPE class could undertake as a result of this visit.

(6 marks)

Anne Frank Information Sheet for Section 2, Question 1.

March 2005: The 60th Anniversary of the death of ANNE FRANK

Anne Frank was born seventy-six years ago on 12th June 1929. She died in Bergen-Belsen concentration camp in Germany in March 1945.

Anne Frank is famous for her diary in which she recorded her life hiding in the Secret Annexe from 1942 until 1944.

The story of Anne Frank still has important lessons to teach us today. The discrimination and racism that brought an end to her life did not disappear with the end of World War II. Reading her life story can help us realise the value of tolerance and respect and the importance of human rights.

Today people are still being persecuted and murdered because they, just like Anne, are different.

At the Anne Frank House museum, keeping the memory of Anne Frank alive is directly connected to the concepts of '*freedom*', '*human rights*' and '*democracy*'.

Student Council Brochure for Section 2, Question 2.

Child Labour Poster for Section 2, Question 3.

Child Labour involves children in the making of bricks, working with machinery in agriculture and carpet weaving, in domestic labour, in the sex industry, in construction work, in deep-sea fishing and in the making of matches and fireworks and hundreds of other activities that deny children the right to full-time education.

1 in every 6 people aged between 5 and 17 years is defined as a child labourer

Trading Fairly Page for Section 2, Question 4.